DESIGNING THE T-34

GENESIS OF THE REVOLUTIONARY SOVIET TANK

Peter Samsonov

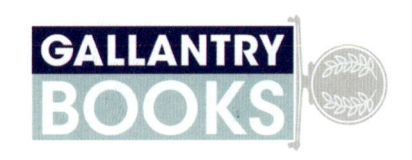

GALLANTRY BOOKS

*Dedicated to my best friend who gave me the
best review I could hope for.*

First published in Great Britain in 2019
by Gallantry Books
an imprint of Mortons Books Ltd.
Media Centre
Morton Way
Horncastle LN9 6JR
www.mortonsbooks.co.uk

Copyright © Gallantry Books, 2019

All rights reserved. No part of this publication may be reproduced or transmitted in any form or by any means, electronic or mechanical including photocopying, recording, or any information storage retrieval system without prior permission in writing from the publisher.

ISBN 978 1 911658 30 6

The right of Peter Samsonov to be identified as the author of this work has been asserted in accordance with the Copyright, Designs and Patents Act 1988.

Typeset by ATG Media

10 9 8 7 6 5 4 3 2 1

Acknowledgements
I would like to thank Aleksey Makarov, Igor Zheltov, Yuri Pasholok, Dmitriy Shein, Andrei Ulanov, Francis Pulham, and Alex Zaretser whose work made this book and many others possible. I would also like to thank Pavel Borovikov for his considerable contribution and support during the writing of this book and Maryse Beauregard for proofreading the finished work.

Contents

Introduction	**6**
Two Tanks for the Price of One	**18**
Bigger and Better	**30**
Colour Profiles	**45**
From A to T	**52**
Production and Service	**75**
Glossary	**85**
Notes	**87**
Index	**90**

Chapter 1
Introduction

"The design shows a clear-headed appreciation of the essentials of an effective tank and the requirements of war, duly adjusted to the particular characteristic of the Russian soldier, the terrain, and the manufacturing facilities available. When it is considered how recently Russia has become industrialized and how great a proportion of the industrialized regions have been over-run by the enemy, with the consequent loss or hurried evacuation of plant and workers, the design and production of such useful tanks in such great numbers stands out as an engineering achievement of the first magnitude."

Preliminary Report #20, Russian T/34, Military College of Science, School of Tank Technology, Chertsey, UK, February 1944

ABOVE: The first mass-production tanks used by the Russian army were foreign designs, supplied by the British and French governments to aid the White Army faction in the Russian Civil War. This tank, General Drozdovskiy, is a British Mark V. Captured Mark V tanks served in the Red Army under the designation 'Ricardo'.
Central Museum of the Armed Forces

Introduction

There are many places that one can choose to start from when telling the story of the T-34 tank. A common starting point is June 22, 1941, the first day of the Great Patriotic War, the first of many battles in the T-34's combat career. Others begin on December 19, 1939, when the Council of People's Commissars of the USSR accepted the tank into service. Some go further back, starting with the development of the A-20 tank. Any of those will do if one is describing what kind of tank the T-34 was. However, in order to understand how and why the T-34 became an engineering achievement of the first magnitude, we must go back even further.

Soviet tank industry was born in war. The first Soviet-built tanks, marginally improved copies of the Renault FT, were

ABOVE: A captured British Medium Tank Mark B with a Worker and Peasant Red Army crew. The tank bears an early design of the red star insignia, featuring a hammer and plough, rather than a sickle.
Central Museum of the Armed Forces

ABOVE: Renault FT tanks being delivered to Russia. This design was considered more promising than captured British tanks, and was used as an inspiration for the earlier generations of Soviet armour.
Central Museum of the Armed Forces

meant to bolster the nascent Worker and Peasant Red Army's stock of tanks captured in the Russian Civil War. Production started while the war was still raging, and only manufacturing delays prevented these 'Russian Renault' tanks from taking part in the hostilities. Without combat experience, it was unclear how the tank could further be improved. As a result, the Red Army's next tank, the MS-1, was conceptually similar to its predecessor. Experience in defending the Chinese Eastern Railway from Chinese warlords showed that the Red Army had a long way to go before it learned to use any tanks effectively, but it was already clear that the tanks themselves left much to be desired.[1] Unfortunately, domestic designers had little experience in tank building, and it was decided that outside help was necessary. In no uncertain terms, the Supreme Soviet of the National Economy and People's Commissariat of Military and Naval Affairs were instructed to "take all measures to use foreign technical aid more widely"[2] by the Council of Labour and Defence during a meeting held on October 13, 1929.

The result of this decision is well known. A purchasing commission was

ABOVE: Although it resembled its French ancestor visually, the MS-1 surpassed it in a number of ways. These tanks were written off in the 1930s and repurposed as pillboxes, which is why all tanks of this type seen today have replica tracks and suspensions.
Central Museum of the Armed Forces

formed and sent abroad, returning with, among other samples, two turretless Christie M.1940 tanks.[3] Despite the tank initially being considered inadequate for service,[4] significant improvements were made to the design over the next several years. By 1934 the BT-5 tank was one of the best tanks in service with the Red Army. With the same armour as the T-26 tank, it was significantly more manoeuvrable. The low lifespan of track links, a defect that plagued most tanks of the era, was mitigated by the fact that the tanks could travel great distances on wheels and only equip their tracks when going into battle. The tanks' great speed also allowed them to be funnelled into breakthroughs and wreck enemy rear echelon forces, making them valuable tools on the battlefield.

The next major shake-up of the Soviet tank industry was the Spanish Civil War. Despite the technical supremacy of Soviet T-26 and BT-5 tanks over German Pz.Kpfw.I tanks and Italian CV 3/35 tankettes,[5] several weaknesses of these

ABOVE: The MS-1 from the front. As there was no coaxial gun mount available at the time, the cannon and machine gun are mounted separately.
Central Museum of the Armed Forces

Introduction

tanks were revealed. Their armour was vulnerable to armour-piercing bullets at point-blank range, not to mention towed 3.7-cm Pak anti-tank guns and 20–25-mm autocannons.[6] The 45-mm cannon did not possess an effective enough high-explosive round, and dealing with fortifications of any kind was difficult. Furthermore, fighting in the city left the tanks vulnerable to attack from above, where bottles filled with petrol or other flammable fluid (later colloquially known as 'Molotov cocktails') could be thrown onto the engine deck, igniting the tanks' engines.

Even though Soviet involvement in the Spanish Civil War lasted until 1938, conclusions from lessons learned in combat were drawn fairly quickly. On March 21, 1937, defence minister Kliment Voroshilov wrote to the Chief of the Automobile, Armoured Vehicle, and Tank Directorate (ABTU), Gustav Gustavovich Bokis:

ABOVE: The T-37A tank also had foreign roots. This tank was based on Vickers-Carden-Loyd designs.
Central Museum of the Armed Forces

BELOW: The T-38 tank was an improvement on the T-37A, but kept the British suspension. T-37A and T-38 tanks were considered obsolete by 1941, and replaced with the T-40, but many of them still fought in the Great Patriotic War. This example was equipped with additional armour and a 20-mm autocannon. These modernized tanks were no longer amphibious.
Central Museum of the Armed Forces

ABOVE: A T-26 infantry support tank, a licensed copy of the Vickers Mark E Type A tank. This variant is upgraded compared to its British relative, and features a 37-mm cannon in one turret. *Patriot Park*

Experience in using the T-26 shows that they are unsuitable for combat in settlements, where these tanks take heavy losses without fail. There is no reason to assume that other tanks will do much better in these conditions. We must have tanks that are specially designed for street fighting, not just in small towns, but in large cities, where the enemy will have the ability to strike the tanks from above, from upper storeys of houses. Discuss this issue (invite Arman and Krivoshein) and report to me within twenty days your ideas about a tank specially designed for street fighting.

Voroshilov's dream street-fighting tank had to be able to destroy stone walls by ramming them with its hull, fire upward at an angle of up to 70 degrees, be protected from penetration by flammable liquids, and have improved protection, specifically thicker front armour and a shielded suspension, all without impacting agility. The tank was required to have a convertible drive, a better design than what BT tanks had at the time. Voroshilov explicitly requested N. F. Tsyganov's BT-IS-style drive with multiple powered wheels on each side.

These suggestions had some traction. On April 8 and 9, 1937, a discussion was held between a number of high-ranking ABTU members and senior staff from factories

#174 and #183. Also present were Semyon Moiseevich Krivoshein, the commander of a Soviet tank group in Spain, and Paul Matisovich Arman, a commander of a tank company, another veteran of Spain, whose service had earned him the title of Hero of the Soviet Union. Mikhail Ilyich Koshkin was also present. Instead of blindly relying on Voroshilov's suggestions, the tank designers decided to get their information straight from the source, but a lot of the conclusions were the same. The Red Army's future tanks had to:

- be able fight both in cities and open fields
- have at least a 76-mm cannon and armour impenetrable to 45-mm armour-piercing shells fired from a range of 1,000 metres
- have 60–70 degrees of gun elevation.

This issue would be attacked from two directions: by means of modernizing existing tanks and by designing a brand-new tank.[7]

Work started almost immediately. At a meeting held on May 7 between the ABTU and head designers of various tank factories, it was established that a modernization of the BT-7, T-46 (the ailing replacement for the T-26) and T-35 that would allow them to elevate their main gun to 70 degrees would be possible by developing new turrets. However, mounting a 76-mm gun in the BT-7 and T-46 would be a difficult task that would require serious modification of the entire tank. This could be done only in BT-7-B-IS and T-46-3 tanks, both of which were currently in development. Two variants of the new-model street-fighting tank were also discussed. One was purely evolutionary, and was essentially an upgraded T-29: a 76-mm gun with the required elevation would be mounted in the main turret, with two miniature turrets carrying 12.7-mm DK machine guns with coaxial 7.62-mm DT machine guns in the front. This tank would have 30 mm of sloped armour and weigh about 30 tons.

ABOVE: The ultimate form of the T-26 featured a 45-mm gun and sloped armour, but the weight climbed to over 10 tons as a result of all these improvements. This tank could no longer be improved without a core redesign. *Kubinka Tank Museum*

RIGHT: An intermediate T-26 model. The biggest change compared to its predecessor was the introduction of one large turret, which became standard on all Soviet light tanks. New features included a coaxial machine-gun mount, a more powerful 45-mm gun and a turret bustle that could house a radio or an ammunition-ready rack. *Central Museum of the Armed Forces*

Designing the T-34

The second idea, an entirely new design, was much more interesting. This tank would be protected with 40–50-mm of sloped armour, and would weigh 25–30 tons. This tank would run on tracks only.[8] Even though the T-34 was still more than two and a half years away, the requirements described here sound awfully familiar.

However, Komkor (Corps Commander) Dmitriy Grigoryevich Pavlov, who became the Deputy Chief (and soon after, Chief) of the ABTU upon his return from Spain, had some different ideas. According to him, modernization of existing tanks was a waste of time. The T-35, the Red Army's biggest and heaviest breakthrough tank, was vulnerable to 37-mm guns, let alone 45-mm ones. Increasing the armour to levels that would make the tank viable on a battlefield saturated with anti-tank artillery would essentially require the design of an entirely new tank. The T-28 was in a similar boat. The T-29, a T-28-like medium tank with a Christie suspension and convertible drive, was also no longer considered suitable for the role it was supposed to play in the Red Army. The BT-7 and T-26 were suitable for their roles, but Pavlov was eager to see them replaced with something more modern. Pavlov's approach was evolutionary, rather than revolutionary, although he was willing to let go of the convertible drive if a tracked tank with a 3,000-km lifespan could be developed. Pavlov also championed the gradual replacement of gasoline engines with diesel ones, at least on fast cavalry-style tanks like the BT, and the adoption of a more powerful 76-mm gun with a muzzle velocity of at least 560 m/s (the KT-28 76.2-mm tank gun in use at the time had a muzzle velocity of only 381 m/s).[9] These suggestions were sent to Voroshilov on February 2, 1938. Voroshilov was interested, and asked for additional documents to prepare a report to the Soviet government. Pavlov's response made on March 14 shaped the fate of the T-34:

There ought to be only one type of tank to accompany infantry/cavalry and serve in independent tank units. Create two types of experimental light tanks: one purely tracked, armed with a 45-mm tank gun and a coaxial machine gun, with armour thick enough to protect from 12.7-mm bullets at all ranges, top speed of 50–60 kph, and a mass of up to 13 tons. The other: convertible drive, six powered wheels, the same armament and armour, 50–60 kph top speed on wheels and tracks, mass of up to 15 tons. Use a diesel engine... Perform trials of both in 1939 and decide which one meets all requirements to replace both the BT and T-26.[10]

Voroshilov agreed wholeheartedly. Committee of Defence decree #478ss, issued on March 17, 1938, repeated the requirements stated in Pavlov's letters nearly word for word.

Not everyone had such well-reasoned ideas. For instance, division commander Kolchigin requested an amphibious tank with a crew of six to eight men that had dual driving controls, an automatic towing system, automatic switching between wheels and tracks, a ramming system, a chainsaw for dealing with fortifications, ability to refuel and restock ammunition while driving, and a 76-mm gun capable of direct and indirect fire, as well as an AA machine gun. This wonder-tank was to weigh 18–20 tons. According to him, "the familiarization of tank designers with this work will raise a number of issues that their design work can solve".[11] Thankfully, it was more rational minds that prevailed.

In the absence of any concrete requirements from the Red Army's generals, the ABTU moved conservatively. On October 13, 1937, the tactical-technical requirements for the BT-20 tank were approved. This tank was described as a "convertible drive tank designed

Introduction

ABOVE: Although not a direct copy of a Vickers product, the T-28 was no doubt inspired by the 16-ton Vickers Medium Tank Mark III. The suspension, on the other hand, has German roots, drawing inspiration from the Grosstraktor. While the armour and armament of the T-28 remained fearsome throughout the 1930s, it had a number of drawbacks, such as its low top speed and low-velocity main gun. Many modernization projects of this tank, including installation of appliqué armour, a higher-velocity 76-mm gun and experimental suspensions were developed. However, by 1941, the tank was obviously obsolete.
Central Museum of the Armed Forces

for mechanized formations and cavalry armoured regiments". Its purpose was not significantly different from that of the existing BT series tanks, but it was an evolutionary step forward. The suspension of the tank remained the same as that of its predecessors, with six powered wheels (three per side) to give it improved off-road mobility without having to equip tracks. The top speed on tracks or on wheels would be the same: 70 kph. The tank was powered by the BD-2 400-hp diesel engine designed at HPZ (Kharkov Locomotive Factory) with provisions for later installing a 600-hp engine. The armament of the tank consisted of either a stabilized 45-mm cannon or a 76-mm cannon, and three machine guns: one coaxial, one in the hull and one in the turret bustle. Every fifth tank would have an AA machine gun mount. A flamethrower for self-defence was also required. The requirement for street fighting made a comeback: the tank would have to be able to raise its guns up 65 degrees (and the AA machine gun to 85 degrees). The armour of the tank was thicker than that of its predecessors: 25 mm in the front, 20 in the turret, 16 along the sides and rear, and 10 mm in the roof and floor. The vertical armour plates had to be installed at an angle of at least 18 degrees. In order to protect the crew from chemical weapons and allow the tank to ford rivers, the hull had to be watertight. This tank would weigh 13–14 tons. The reliability requirements were very strict: 300 hours of driving or 5,000 km until refurbishment. Interestingly enough, the departure from the Christie suspension was already considered at this point: the requirements stated that a torsion bar suspension was desirable.[12]

The Red Army's new generation medium tank was no great leap forward either. Initially ordered in 1933, the T-29, was

13

very similar in its characteristics to the T-28 tank, but was equipped with a Christie suspension. The tank had more armour than the original T-28 (30–40 mm in the front), but not a lot more, certainly not enough to take anti-tank gun fire at close range. Only a small note in the approved requirements hinted at the future development of Soviet medium tanks: "Consider potentially transitioning to a diesel engine in 1939."[13] Stalingrad Tractor Factory (STZ) was also instructed to "in parallel, without taking time from your primary tasks, work on the issue of transitioning from a gasoline engine to diesel".[14]

The idea that the Soviet defence industry was a homogeneous, well-oiled machine is common in the West. However, that was far from the case. As with any complex procurement project, something like the new tank required cooperation of a great number of organizations, both military and civilian, who had their own priorities and at the end of the day had to look after their own people first and foremost. The creation of a new type of BT tank was not considered an exceptionally high priority project, at least by factory #183, which was tasked with its development. Due to the factory's abysmal showing in designing the BT-IS tank just earlier that year, ABTU Chief Bokis suggested the creation of a brand-new design group within the factory. This group would be subordinated directly to the factory's chief engineer, and headed by Military Engineer 3rd Class Adolf Yakovlevich Dik, an adjunct from the Tank and Tractor faculty of the Military Academy of Motorization and Mechanization (VAMM). This group would be staffed by 30 diploma students from the VAMM, increased to 50 on December 1, 1937. Factory #183 would have to provide support staff and living quarters for the arriving students, as well as eight of its own engineers to lead teams of these newly minted designers. Dik arrived at factory #183 on October 1 only to find out that the factory's management not only had no interest in assembling a special design bureau, but in working on the new BT tank at all. Unable to get anything done, Dik

BELOW: T-29 medium tank. This tank was more mobile than the T-28, but its potential was hampered by the archaic multi-turreted design. The T-29 could not meet the requirements for the Red Army's next generation medium tank. *Patriot Park*

Introduction

departed on October 18, and Bokis wrote an enraged letter to Mikhail Moiseevich Kaganovich, the People's Commissar of Defence Industry, demanding that urgent measures be taken to get the project off the ground.

The situation looked dire indeed: two months had passed since the new BT tank was ordered, but work had not yet begun in any capacity. Serious organizational measures were taken to resolve this problem. K. P. Farmanyants, the chief of the 8th department of the People's Commissariat of Defence Industry (NKOP), was bumped down to deputy chief, his role taken by D. V. Sviridov. Sviridov and Bokis met with factory #183 director Bondarenko on October 29, 1937, to discuss the creation of the special design bureau. The bureau would have been a pretty powerful entity: not only would it take the best designers the factory employed (selected by Dik), but also ten additional designers, 40 students from the VAMM, and the entirety of workshop #191. These resources would be freed from any current production work and focus entirely on the new tank under Dik's supervision. Bondarenko refused: according to him, the head of the special design bureau should be an engineer from the factory, not a temporary visitor from another organization.

ABOVE: The BT-2 tank was famously inspired by the Christie tank purchased by the USSR. The hull was largely based off Christie's prototype, but the turret was a new Soviet design. Like the T-26, the tank has a 37-mm cannon and a machine gun, but both weapons are mounted separately since a coaxial mount was not available. This specific exhibit consists of a BT-2 turret on a BT-5 hull. *Patriot Park*

LEFT: The BT-5 was the successor to the BT-2, featuring a number of improvements. This tank was also equipped with a larger turret and a more powerful 45-mm gun, the same type of turret used on the T-26. *Patriot Park*

Bondarenko had his way. 'Bureau #24', created in the first half of November, was headed by Mikhail Ilyich Koshkin, previously the head of design bureau #190. Alexander Alexandrovich Morozov was selected as his deputy. Koshkin agreed with the need to separate his workers from any other production. Bureau #24 was set up behind closed doors. Entry to the design bureau's offices was barred to other factory staff, even high-ranking designers and engineers. In addition to protecting his tank from spies, Koshkin also protected his team from distractions.

The factory's manufacturing base was expanded as well. Workshop #191 was a rather small part of the factory, and Sviridov suggested to Kaganovich that 3–4 million rubles should be spent on its expansion.

Work began on November 15 with 18 designers, but the amount fluctuated during the development of the tank. Only 16 staff (six engineers and ten technicians) were left on January 1, 1938, and the number increased to 19 by March 5 (ten engineers, nine technicians, one copier, and one secretary). This was a far cry from the 50-person design bureau that Dik envisioned, and entirely unsatisfactory even by the factory director's Bondarenko's estimate, who considered that this sort of work should be performed by 33 engineers.[15]

Despite this shortage, the project was coming to an end by this time. On March 9, 1938, Bondarenko sent a telegram to the ABTU requesting a commission for the review and approval of the draft project. The project was submitted on March 17, 1938, and reviewed by the ABTU in Moscow on March 25. The tank that was presented weighed 16 tons, significantly higher than expected.[16] Despite this, the ABTU deemed this tank generally satisfactory, but not before presenting Koshkin's team with a laundry list of design changes. The maximum weight of the tank was increased to 15.5 tons to allow for all of the desired

ABOVE: The BT-7 started to push the limits of modernizing the Christie chassis. Despite aims to install a 76-mm gun in this tank, most BT-7 tanks were built with the same 45-mm gun as the BT-5.
Central Museum of the Armed Forces

ABOVE: Unlike British cruiser tanks that evolved from the Christie design, the BT series retained the ability to switch between tracks and wheels. This meant that the front pair of wheels had to turn in order to steer the tank, limiting the amount of space available in the driver's compartment and creating the characteristic pointed-nose shape.
Central Museum of the Armed Forces

improvements.[17] However, Pavlov, the new ABTU chief, scolded Bondarenko for taking seven months to produce as much as a draft, reminding him that the new tank needed to be in production by January 1, 1939, and that time was ticking.[18] This work was important enough that Sviridov was willing to transfer more manpower to the project. He ordered 11 designers transferred internally from other factory #183 design departments, three from factory #185, and two from factory #37. These were temporary assignments, and factory #183 would be paying for their lodgings.[19]

Discussion between the army and the engineers continued, and the ABTU changed the requirements again on May 13, 1938. According to the document, titled 'Brief tactical-technical characteristics of the BT-20 convertible drive tank', the front armour of the new tank would be composed of a 30-mm plate at 30 degrees and a 20-mm plate at 53 degrees. This would be enough to protect it from 12.7-mm armour-piercing bullets. The gun mantlet had to be thick enough to withstand being hit by a 37-mm shell. The crew was increased to four tankers, unlike the tank's predecessors, all of which had three crewmen. The new crew member would operate the radio and fire the hull machine gun. The requirement for a rear-mounted flamethrower was removed. The required top speed was 65 kph, and the tank now required a 500-hp engine. The armament of the tank would be a 45- or 76-mm gun with an Orion stabilizer, which would allow for accurate fire at a speed of up to 30 kph. The gun elevation requirement was reduced to a more reasonable 45 degrees. The weight limit of the tank was raised to 16.5 tons. Reliability requirements were lowered to 300 hours or 3,000 km until refurbishment.[20]

The requirements were changing so quickly that they were never composed into one complete document, much to the annoyance of factory #183's new director, Parfenov. Thankfully, the military did not expect his designers to do the impossible. On August 21, 1938, NKOP order #335ss gave a new deadline: the factory was to produce one convertible drive and two tracked tanks (one of them with a flamethrower) by June 1, 1939, instead of the previous deadline, which required the new tank to be in production by January 1, 1939.[21]

BELOW: A column of Soviet armoured vehicles in Bessarabia, 1940. A T-26 leads the charge. The vast majority of tanks in the Red Army were equipped with 45-mm cannons and bulletproof armour, and even the most optimistic rearmament plans did not project a complete replacement of these old models with modern tanks earlier than 1942 or 1943.
Central Museum of the Armed Forces

Designing the T-34

Chapter 2
Two Tanks for the Price of One

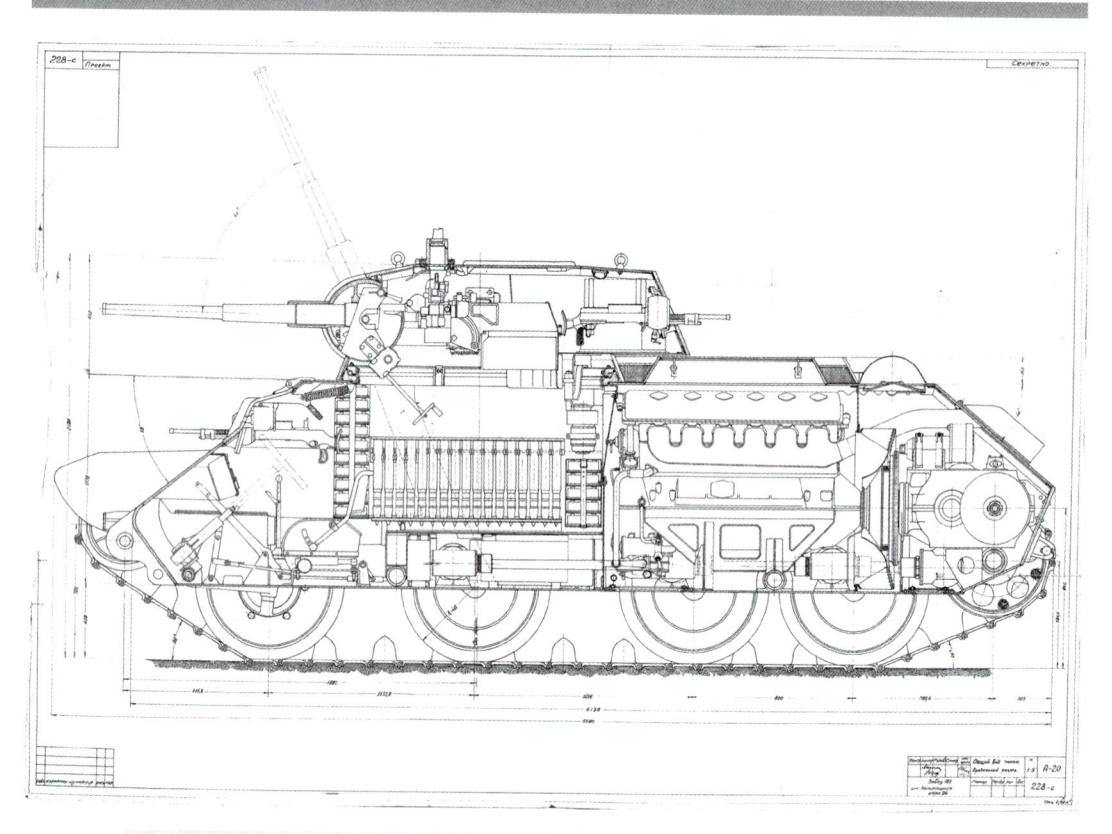

ABOVE: The first iteration of the A-20 tank. Note the extreme gun elevation and rear-facing machine gun. These features were added to the list of requirements as a result of experience in the Spanish Civil War. The final T-34 design lacked both of these features.
Personal collection of Aleksey Makarov

> "Only the USSR exploited the genius of American tank designer Walter Christie, whose inventions underwrote World War II's best tank, the Soviet T-34."
>
> 'U.S. Intelligence and Soviet Armor',
> Major General Paul F. Gorman

A revised project was presented for approval on August 27, 1938. The BT-20, now exclusively referred to as the A-20, changed beyond recognition. The mass of the tank reached 17 tons, but this was a small price to pay for the radically increased protection afforded by a new hull shape, which featured sloped armour all around, not just in the front. The top speed of the tank was the same on either tracks or wheels: 65 kph. This allowed running the tank with only one track installed. The transmission and running gear components were based on those used in earlier BT tanks, but were improved in various ways. The final drive was an exception, and was an entirely new design. Track links were also based on the BT series links, but were 70 mm wider. With two more links per track (72 total), this amounted to an increase in weight of 220 kg (1,049 kg in total) for both tracks. The memo attached to the design proposal explains that these track links proved themselves satisfactory when tested on BT tanks, showing a lifespan of over 2,000 km. The fighting compartment was widened at the cost of increasing the turning radius of the tank on wheels, as the wheel could turn at a shallow angle. The tank lost the characteristic pointed shape of the BT hull.

The hull of the tank was entirely welded, with the exception of armour plates that could be removed to access the engine and transmission, which were held on by bolts. The front armour was 20 mm thick, but presented at an angle of 53 degrees (top section) or 70.5 degrees (bottom section). The rounded part of the front had an additional 10 mm of armour welded over it. The formerly vertical sides were now 20 mm thick and angled at 35 degrees above track level. Vertical side armour behind the wheels was 25 mm thick. The driver's cabin, now greatly reduced in size and built into the driver's hatch, had a 25-mm-thick front at an angle of 25 degrees. The thicker armour came at a cost of weight: the weight of the hull armour increased to 4,650 kg (compared to 2,400 kg on the BT-7). However, the hull was much simpler to produce, partially because extra ribs to improve rigidity of the hull could be done away with now that the hull itself was much thicker. The tank had more protection than just armour: louvres on the air intakes could be closed by the driver to protect the internal components of the tank from shell splinters, bullets or flammable liquid.

The turret also changed compared to the BT-7. The sides of the turret were 25 mm thick, angled at 20 degrees. A 71-TK radio was installed in the turret bustle. The turret could be turned by either hand or motorized traverse. A 45-mm gun with a coaxial machine gun was used, aimed via a periscopic or telescopic sight (only the periscopic sight could be used at high elevations), stabilized with the experimental Orion vertical stabilizer. The gun could elevate up to an impressive 65 degrees and depress down to -7 degrees. No ammunition was held in the turret. Twenty rounds were stored along each side of the fighting compartment, with 120 more rounds in

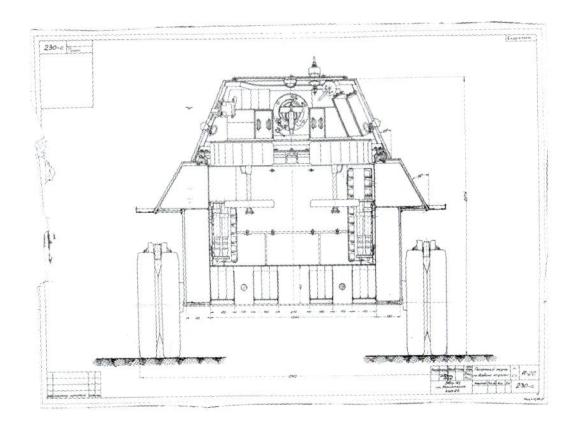

ABOVE: The first iteration of the A-20 tank. The tank was already visually similar to the final T-34, featuring sloped hull and turret armour to improve protection.
Personal collection of Aleksey Makarov

ABOVE: A-20 tank, as produced in metal. Even though the upper hull is very different from its predecessors, the turret is somewhat reminiscent of late-model T-26 and BT-7 turrets. Similar to the BT series, the tank had four large road wheels per side. *RGVA*

ABOVE: A-20 tank, viewed from the rear. The rear of the tank is radically different from its predecessor, despite using the same V-2 engine as the BT-7M. *RGVA*

four-round cases on the floor. Twenty-three machine-gun magazines of 63 rounds each were stored under the floor of the fighting compartment and 23 more in the sponson on the right side. Including the magazine loaded into each machine gun, this added up to a total of 48 magazines, or 3,024 rounds.

The hatches and joints of the tank were airtight to resist chemical weapons and allow the tank to cross water hazards. The maximum depth the tank could submerge to was 5 metres, provided air could enter the tank through a hose.

As interesting as this new tank was, the real gem came after. Attachment #1 to this proposal contained specifications for another tank, called A-20 (tracked). The A-20 (tracked) was largely identical to the A-20, but did not have a convertible drive. As a result, the tank weighed 700 kg less than its wheeled counterpart. The removal of the turning mechanisms allowed the designers to widen the hull by 122 mm, improving crew conditions. The design of the ammunition racks was also simplified, allowing the tank to carry more ammunition: 136 rounds on the floor, 20 on each side, and 24 under the seats, for a total of 200 45-mm shells. The amount of machine-gun ammunition carried also increased by ten magazines to 3,654 rounds in total. An idea of equipping the tank with a 76.2-mm L-10 gun instead of a 45-mm gun was also proposed. This change could be made while staying under the 17-ton limit.[22] This gun could penetrate 40 mm of armour at a 30-degree angle from 500 metres, which was enough to defeat any known enemy tank.[23] The semi-automatic breech and increased muzzle velocity made it significantly more effective than the 76-mm model 1927/32 tank gun in service at the time.

The model commission sent to factory #183 was intrigued by this new proposal. After reviewing the presented materials, a recommendation was given on September 6, 1938, to produce one convertible drive tank with a 45-mm gun, two tracked tanks with 76-mm guns and one hull to perform penetration trials. Some design changes were suggested. The armour would have to be thickened: the fighting compartment floor from 10-mm to 13-mm, and the driver's cabin from 25 mm to 30 mm. The 76-mm gun version of the tank would carry 85–100 rounds of ammunition for the cannon. Another suggestion was to implement pneumatic servo controls that were being tested on BT-7 tanks at the time.[24] These suggestions were implemented quickly: the pneumatic servos were added to the design in early October. The project was reviewed and accepted on October 14. However, there was a cost to this change: the servo mechanism was very heavy, and the weight limit for the A-20 was still strictly 16.5 tons.

ABOVE: The L-10 76.2-mm gun had highly performing armour-piercing and high-explosive ammunition, making it effective against enemy tanks, personnel and even light fortifications. *RGVA*

ABOVE: The DT (Dyegtyaryev Tankoviy) 7.62-mm machine gun with a 63-round disk magazine. This type of machine gun was installed in a tank in either a fixed mount as a coaxial gun or ball mount in the hull or turret. A pintle mount for anti-aircraft use was also introduced. The collapsible stock allowed the crew to remove the gun and use it for self-defence if they had to bail out of the tank. Introduced in 1929, the DT remained the standard tank machine gun until the end of World War II. *RGVA*

ABOVE: The A-32 tank, initially pitched under the name 'A-20 (tracked)'. The layout of the hull was similar to the A-20, but the enlarged turret fitted a 76-mm L-10 gun and the number of road wheels per side was increased from four to five. *RGVA*

ABOVE: The A-32 from the rear. The rear hull was the same as the A-20, and only the extra road wheel distinguishes this tank from its competitor at this angle. *RGVA*

Koshkin's team worked all autumn to implement the changes proposed by the model commission. On December 9/10, 1938, Koshkin and Morozov travelled to Moscow to present their project at a meeting of the Supreme Military Council of the Red Army. Wooden models and documents on the A-20 and A-20 (tracked) were presented to an audience of high-ranking officers and party officials, including Stalin, Lev Mekhlis, Voroshilov and Semyon Budyonny. According to Morozov's memoirs, the majority of the participants favoured the convertible drive variant, but Stalin himself stepped in, saying: "Let's not get in the designers' way. Let them make the tank they propose, and we'll see if it's really as good as they say."

This quote, combined with another suggestion to "not stifle the factory's initiative" is interpreted in some sources as a suggestion that the A-20 (tracked) was developed by Bureau #24 on their own accord. That is not the case, as the NKOP explicitly ordered the development of a tracked tank on August 21, 1938.

It was hard to argue with Stalin, and the commission concluded that one of each tank would be built. The requirements remained largely the same. The required gun elevation was further reduced to 25–30 degrees, with gun depression remaining at -7 degrees. The weight limit was set at 16.5 tons for the convertible drive tank and 17 tons for the tracked tank. However, the heavier tank had to have a lower ground pressure: 0.5 cm/kg^2, compared to the lighter tank's 0.57 cm/kg^2, both significantly lower than the calculated ground pressure of the existing design (0.65 cm/kg^2). The armour requirements were left rather vague: "protection from large-calibre 12.7-mm armour-piercing bullets at all ranges". According to Pavlov, the existing armour was not enough, and he suggested that the vertical sides ought to be 30 mm thick, which would have made achieving the weight and ground pressure requirements even harder. The ammunition storage requirement was taken as the minimum recommended previously: 85 rounds of ammunition for the 76-mm gun or 150 rounds for the 45-mm gun.[25]

ABOVE: An A-20 descends a 37-degree slope during trials. Army trials included driving over varied types of difficult terrain in order to determine the limits of the tank's mobility. *RGVA*

Bureau #24 had a lot of work to do to meet these new requirements. A report by factory #183's ABTU representative stated that the factory was still at work on the project as of January 1, 1939. The plan was to complete the hull and turret blueprints first so that armour components could be ordered by the end of January. The bureau was still understaffed: only 29 workers (25 designers and four copiers) instead of the requisite thirty-seven. It's no wonder that the development of a number of components was behind schedule.

Thankfully, the bureau was given a break by an unexpected turn of bureaucracy. On January 11, 1939, the massive NKOP was decomposed into a number of commissariats: Aircraft Production, Shipbuilding, Ammunition and Armament. A similar decomposition occurred soon after: on February 5, 1939, the People's Commissariat of Machine Building (NKMash) was split into three: People's Commissariats of Heavy, Medium and General Machine

Building. Factory #183 and the 8th department initially ended up under the umbrella of the People's Commissariat of Aircraft Production, and was later moved into the People's Commissariat of Medium Machine Building (NKSM). In this bureaucratic maelstrom, even such a trivial task as presenting the requirements already approved by the Military Council to the Committee of Defence took several months. Luckily for bureau #24, the requirements were approved unanimously on February 27 by Committee of Defence decree #45ss.[26] These requirements were passed down to the People's Commissar of Medium Machine Building, Ivan Alekseevich

ABOVE: An A-20 climbs a 1.1-metre-high wall. Barricades were effective anti-tank measures in city fighting, and it was important to make sure that tanks could climb over considerable obstacles without assistance. *RGVA*

ABOVE: An A-20 drives at a 10-degree tilt with only one track installed. The ability to drive with one side using tracks and the other using wheels was an important requirement for the A-20, as destroying a track was a very common way of disabling a tank without penetrating its armour. *RGVA*

ABOVE: An A-20 climbs a 40-degree slope during trials. Trials like these revealed what limited the tank's off-road mobility: engine power or traction between the tracks and the ground. Weaknesses such as tracks slipping off would also be revealed in trials like these. *RGVA*

Likhachev, who, in turn, gave order #22ss on March 17. This order repeated the existing requirements and ordered Aleksey Adamovich Goreglyad, the new head of the 8th department, to report on the progress of these projects every month. Delays were not acceptable. Personnel responsible for various parts of the project, both within the factory and subcontractors, were to be identified to Likhachev by name so that any delays could be quickly resolved.[27]

The deadline was approaching quickly. Factory management finally decided to take action and correct bureau #24's staffing issue. A number of personnel were transferred from other design groups. The post of Chief Engineer of the Factory was also created. On April 1, 1939, a proposal was made to give this role to Koshkin. He was appointed to it by mid-May. At the same time, Morozov stepped up as the head of the enlarged design bureau, now bearing the index #520. Around this time the name of the A-20 (tracked) was changed to A-32. The name A-20G was also used.

However, management is one thing, but actual production is another. Due to scheduling and production issues at the Mariupol factory, the two A-32 hulls arrived at factory #183 only on April 30, but they did not have sides installed. Those would only be sent out later.[28] Production of the armour was only completed on May 11.[29]

Factory #183 wasn't any better at keeping on schedule: as of May 4, 1939, blueprints for eight assemblies had not yet been completed, and the only assembly actually built was one brake band. Radical measures were taken to get the project back on track: the schedule of the manufacturing workshop responsible for the prototypes changed to three shifts around the clock. Production of A-20 components had the highest priority, even higher than spare parts for existing tanks. These measures paid off, and assembly of the A-20 soon reached the point where it could drive on its own. A 1-km-long test drive was made within the factory on wheels in first and second gear on May 26. The tank was still missing a number of parts, including weapons. Complete assembly was expected on May 29.[30]

The A-20 took its first steps outside the factory on June 1, 1939. A 174-km march revealed that the prototype suffered from a number of water, oil and fuel leaks, which were corrected when the tank returned from its test run. The impressions given by the crew were encouraging: the driver reported

ABOVE: Another hazard encountered in city fighting is petrol bombs or Molotov cocktails thrown by enemy soldiers hiding in upper floors of buildings. The A-20 was covered in gasoline and set ablaze to test its resistance to this type of attack. *RGVA*

ABOVE: An A-32 is crossing a 1.4-metre-deep river during trials. Being able to ford a deep river independently was advantageous, as the enemy would no doubt attempt to destroy any bridges capable of carrying a tank during a retreat. *RGVA*

ABOVE: An A-32 attempting to cross a 0.7-metre-deep swamp. The wide tracks and low ground pressure of the tank allowed it to cross ground that was impossible for other tanks to drive over, which allowed Soviet tank units to deliver surprise attacks from unexpected directions. *RGVA*

that the tank was easy to steer and smooth to drive. The commander agreed that the test vehicle behaved well. Without tracks, machine guns, crewmen, observation devices and some of the ammunition, the tank weighed in at 15,840 kg. It was estimated that the fully stowed tank would weigh 17,770 kg.

The tank made another outing on June 4, driving for 175 km, this time on tracks. No defects were discovered, but a note was made that this time the gearbox and final drives heated up more than in the previous trials. The tank returned to the workshop to complete assembly by June 13.[31] The full trials programme was received on the same day. Both the A-20 and A-32 would be facing a 2,500-km course: 700 on a cobblestone road, 1,000 on dirt roads and 800 km off-road. A full obstacle course would also be a part of the trials, including smashing through walls, navigating dense forests and crossing difficult terrain, such as swamps and moats.[32] The trials were scheduled to start on June 27, but it was not to be. The A-20 was still not completely assembled by July 2: the tank was missing its Orion stabilizer and radio. However, the tank was not sitting idle, and continued to run trials even in its incomplete state. By this time it had driven 700 km. Minor issues were detected and corrected.[33] The tank ran another 100 km by July 6, this time over more difficult terrain. Comparative trials with BT-7 and BT-7M tanks showed positive results: the older tanks became bogged down in a section of the course with loose dirt and tall grass, but the A-20 managed to cross that area with no issues. The A-20 also easily navigated sandy hills, while the BT-7M had its tracks jam in the same conditions. During high-speed fording trials the A-20 became bogged down and the engine stalled. After spending between two and a half and three hours in the water the tank was evacuated, cleaned out by the crew and managed the drive back to the factory on its own. After these trials another set of minor issues had to be corrected, but the results were encouraging: the tank was clearly a significant improvement over its predecessor. Despite the increased weight it was quick and agile: the testers measured a top speed of 85 kph.

As trials of the A-20 progressed, the A-32 programme stalled. Despite the effort that the engineers put into defending the A-32, the tank didn't seem like anyone's top priority. On May 26 Mariupol factory reported that assembly of the A-32 (referred to as the 'A-20 second variant' in the report) was delayed and the hull would not be ready before May 30. This estimate proved correct. The hull had arrived on May 31 and was ready for cutting. It was estimated that assembly would only start on June 6 and would be completed by June 10–13.[34] Even that proved to be an optimistic evaluation.

On June 13, the expected completion date moved to the 15th/16th.[35] By July 2 the tank was still not complete, but was capable of driving, having already clocked 110 km on the road, during which a significant leak was discovered. Progress on the second A-32 (referred to in the report as 'vehicle 32') hull was also reported: it would be ready no sooner than July 6.[36]

Four days later, the A-32 was still not fully equipped (ammunition racks were missing), but had travelled another 240 km. The results were also quite impressive: the agility in sand was as good as that of the A-20. The A-32 could climb a 40.5-degree hill, and even that was not its limit of its abilities.

However, these tests were a fraction of what the new prototypes were going to go through in military trials. The new tanks would not be tested alone. As in factory trials, BT-7 and BT-7M tanks would accompany them to see just how much of

ABOVE: An A-20 knocks down an oak tree with a 330-mm-thick trunk. Being able to drive through a thick forest also allowed the tanks to strike from unexpected directions. The turret is turned backward in order to protect the gun barrel from damage. *RGVA*

an improvement over older designs the A-20 and A-32 were.[37] Pavlov's list of requirements, described above, required trials to begin on June 27 and conclude by July 25,[38] but delays in manufacturing shifted that deadline. In actuality, the trials would only begin on July 18. The two tanks drove along nearly the same route: the A-20 drove for 182 km and the A-32 for 184. The performance of the two tanks on tracks was similar. The A-20 was slightly faster (average speed of 35.8 kph vs the A-32's 34.1), but also heated up more due to leaks in the cooling system. The next day was spent on inspecting and servicing the tanks, and on July 20 they set out again, this time accompanied by BT-7 and BT-7M tanks. The four tanks were tested on a highway, where the situation was the opposite of what was seen in mud and sand. Out of the four tanks, the BT-7M accelerated the fastest, reaching a speed of 60 kph in only 14 seconds. The BT-7 was not far behind at 15 seconds, but the significantly heavier A-20 and A-32 took longer to get up to speed at 25 and 32 seconds respectively. The tanks alternated maintenance and trials well into August. Special trials began on August 7. The tanks were driven up hills, along inclines, through swamps and in various other difficult conditions in order to determine off-road mobility. Other systems, such as the cooling system and turning mechanisms, were also put through intensive trials to determine the limits of their operation. Special trials and regular marches continued until August 23, 1939. By the end of the trials, the A-32 had travelled for 3,121 km, and the A-20 for 4,139 km (1,239 on wheels, 2,831 on tracks, and 69 on one track). A repeat of the drag race held at the start of the trials showed that the wear on the tanks was significant. Even though both tanks went above and beyond

BELOW: An A-32 crests a hill during trials. Despite being heavier than the A-20, it still demonstrated exceptional mobility. *RGVA*

the expected trial mileage, this was not the end of their trials.

On that same day, a message came from Likhachev that factory #183's new tanks were to be sent to Moscow for a demonstration to the government. This included the A-20 and A-32. As the tanks were heavily worn from trials, the next 12 days were spent on repairs. Brand-new engines were installed.

On September 5, 1939, the tanks were sent to Kubinka. A demonstration for high-ranking army and government officials, including Voroshilov, Andrei Zhdanov, Anastas Mikoyan and Pavlov, was held on September 22. The tanks successfully navigated the obstacle course. A draft decree was prepared on September 25 for Voroshilov to sign. The decree accepted both the A-20 and A-32 into service. A pilot batch of ten A-20 tanks was due by January 1, 1940, and full-scale production was to begin at factory #183 on March 1.

The case of the A-32 was more complicated. The aforementioned suggestion to thicken the armour was approved. The A-32 was now to be produced with 45 mm of hull armour, and the more powerful and more reliable F-32 76.2-mm gun instead of the L-10. A batch of ten A-32 tanks with the new hull was due on June 1, 1940. Mass production was to start at the Stalingrad Tractor Factory (STZ) on the same day. Voroshilov agreed, and the draft was forwarded to Molotov with nearly no edits, on September 27, 1939.[39] Both the A-20 and A-32 were accepted into production, but the emphasis was clearly shifting towards the A-32. Voroshilov struck out the initial proposal of 15 pilot A-20 tanks and five A-32s in favour of ten of each type of tank.[40]

BELOW: An A-32 is trailed by a thick plume of dust and exhaust on its way up a 37-degree hill during trials. Tanks were tested in harsh, dusty conditions in order to push their air filtration and cooling systems to the limit. *RGVA*

Designing the T-34

Chapter 3

Bigger and Better

ABOVE: The second A-32 prototype loaded with dummy weights to simulate the weight of extra armour. Unlike the first prototype, this tank is equipped with a 45-mm gun. *RGVA*

"We cannot crank out military vehicles indefinitely. These are not tractors. We cannot crush them with numbers. We need to surpass the current level of vehicles, make the enemy's tanks impotent on the battlefield … Quality is the path to supremacy."

V. A. Malyshev

There was a very good reason why production of the A-32 was initially scheduled to start three months after the A-20. The production variant of the A-20 would have been only slightly different from the prototype tank. The A-32, however, was destined for greater things. Since the tank proved much more agile than was required during the initial factory trials, Pavlov decided to make good use of that extra muscle.

On July 6, 1939, orders were given to perform calculations for installing extra armour. An increase of armour thickness of 5 mm all round on the A-20 would result in an increase in weight of 700–750 kg, and an increase of 10 mm on the A-32 would result in a weight increase of 1,600–1,650 kg. The total weight would jump up to 19.5–19.6 tons, but the trade-off would be a tank that was proof against not only heavy machine guns, but even light anti-tank artillery.[41]

A 1.5-ton increase in weight could noticeably affect its mobility characteristics. Rolling and welding thicker armour could introduce complications into the manufacturing process. It was necessary to test these changes and make corrections to the design before production could begin, and time was short. Thankfully, the process began even before the final decision was made by the NKO. On August 18, 1939, Major I. G. Panov reported from factory #183:

> A-32 #2. Currently being assembled. Will be ready on August 25–26. Will be loaded to 21.5–22 tons and put through trials 1,000–1,200 km in length, plus special trials. Trials will begin on August 27 and finish on September 5.
> I gave an order through the factory director to perform weight calculations for 45-mm side armour, 35-mm sponsons, front, rear, etc. We will increase the weight and determine necessary design changes.[42]

BELOW: The same tank from the rear. This tank was indistinguishable from its predecessor aside from its armament. *RGVA*

Designing the T-34

ABOVE: The second A-32 prototype from the right side. No stowage was fitted along the sides of the tank, as all the available space was needed to carry dummy weights. *RGVA*

Due to delays in the assembly, the trials began later than expected, on October 14, and lasted until November 17, 1939. Since the second A-32 prototype was not expected to go through full trials, it was missing a number of components, and a 45-mm gun was installed instead of a 76-mm gun. This tank was loaded with dummy weights, bringing its total mass to 24 tons. During the trials, the tank travelled for 1,534 km, and its engine ran for 61 hours and 3 minutes. The conclusions reflected in the next monthly report were generally positive. The extra weight did not increase oscillations during motion and the tank remained stable while driving on bumpy roads. Pneumatic servos installed on the vehicle made it easy to control. Breakdowns of the gearbox and cooling fan during the trials were determined to be

ABOVE: An A-34 tank from the right side. The A-34 tank already looked quite similar to the T-34, but the design still changed noticeably before mass production. *RGVA*

ABOVE: From the front, the A-34 can be distinguished by one headlight in the upper right of the glacis plate and a large cabin for the driver. A floodlight is installed on top of the cannon for shooting at night. *RGVA*

ABOVE: The rear plate has no hinges, unlike the mass-production T-34. The engine louvre cover also reaches deeper down than on production tanks. *RGVA*

ABOVE: The L-11 gun, seen from the gunner's side, showing the padded recoil guard. The gun had the same ballistics as the F-32 gun, but was not as reliable. Unfortunately, delays in F-32 production left the designers no choice. *RGVA*

LEFT: The L-11 gun, seen from the loader's side. The tray for catching spent shell casings and the canvas sack underneath are shown. *RGVA*

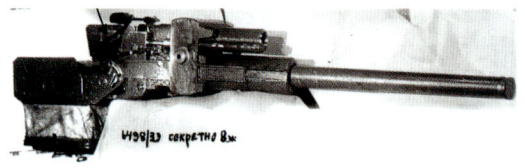

due to manufacturing, rather than design defects. The report concluded that the extra armour was very much worth the effort and suggested a number of minor changes to compensate for the weight.[43]

While the tank with dummy weights was going through trials, assembly of a real one was ordered. On September 28, 1939, the ABTU signed a contract for the production of two tanks with improved armour. Even though the tank was still scheduled to be produced at STZ, this contract was signed with factory #183. The due date on this contract was January 15, 1940. Along with the improved armour, the tank received a new name: A-34. There are a few myths associated with the reason for the new index, but the truth is rather simple: 34 was the next available index for prototypes tested at the factory. A-33 was taken by a halftrack on the ZIS-5 truck chassis.[44]

Having bought some time, factory #183 began fighting to keep its tank. Factory director Yuri Evgeniyevich Maksarev petitioned the ABTU to argue on their behalf. According to Maksarev's calculations, factory #183 could produce the A-32 in the required numbers starting in the second half of 1940. However, the A-20 could not be produced, as it was too complex. There was also a third option: parallel production of the A-20 and A-32, in which case factory #183 would have to be freed from any other contracts. Pavlov was swayed by this argument, commenting that the A-20 must replace the BT and the A-32 would replace the T-26 and T-28. In his vision, this system of armament would last the Red Army another ten years, and should be implemented as quickly as possible. However, the government moved slowly, and the process dragged on for several months.[45]

Meanwhile, factory #183 sprang into action. Cancellation of the archaic T-35 tank freed up a large number of employees, which were funnelled into design bureau #520. The timing was impeccable, as it turned out that the implementation of all required improvements into the A-32 would raise its weight by 6.5 tons. In addition, a number of solutions that worked on the A-32 (for instance, the side of the turret was welded together from two pieces) wouldn't work on the heavier tank. The eight different design groups that worked on the A-34 had a lot of work to do if they wanted to deliver their new tank on time. Blueprints for components ordered from other factories were made first in order to allow them to start work as soon as possible, but even that was often not fast enough. For instance, the Mariupol factory received blueprints for the hull and turret on October 19, 1939, but the armour needed was much thicker than they were used to producing. Preparing the tooling and processes for producing 35-, 40- and 45-mm-thick plates took time, especially for the front plate of the tank, which had to be bent into shape using a 3,000-ton press. Luckily, the Mariupol factory already had a steel alloy suitable for these parts. A cheap and effective type of armour was developed at this factory for 20-mm-thick plates in 1937. Decreasing the amount of carbon and increasing the amount of nickel resulted in high-quality armour that could withstand being hit with 37- and 45-mm shells without cracking or spalling, even when the plates were hardened to high hardness. This alloy was adopted under the index MZ-2.[46]

Conclusions from the trials of the A-32 with dummy weights were put to good use by the designers at bureau #520. The main clutch was simplified, and the number of friction disks was increased from 16 to 22. The gear ratios of the gearbox were changed in order to more rationally use the power of the V-2 engine. The top speed in fourth gear was reduced from 84.26 kph to 53.85 kph. The track contact surface was lengthened by 115 mm, and the width of the track links increased from 400 to 550 mm to keep ground pressure down despite the increased weight.

ABOVE: An A-34 tank drives through a forest barricade. Extra weight and a more powerful engine made it better at smashing through obstacles than any tanks previously employed by the Red Army. *RGVA*

The Mariupol factory completed the two hulls and turrets, as well as proof plates for trials, by the end of November. However, this learning experience was mixed. On one hand, the MZ-2 steel proved to be easy to handle, harden and bend. On the other hand, the factory was ill prepared for mass production. According to factory staff, the production of the parts was "half-improvised, requiring disproportionate amounts of time and effort spent on adapting existing equipment".[47]

To keep the assembly of the prototypes moving as fast as possible, blueprints were submitted into production as they were completed, instead of all at once. This did not help matters significantly. Even though production of individual components was well underway by the middle of November, the project was noticeably behind schedule. Arrival of the armour produced at Mariupol factory was scheduled for December 2, but necessary components would not have been ready in time to begin assembly. Potential delays were identified with components sourced from third parties, but factory #183 had its own problems, as a large amount of equipment needed for A-34 parts was being used to produce BT-7 components to meet the annual quota. Assembly of individual components only began on December 20, less than a month before the A-34 prototype was due for delivery.[48]

Assembly of the hull had begun by December 23, but there was another issue. The requirements for the A-34 tank stated that the tank was supposed to be equipped with the F-32 gun. However, this was news to Koshkin and his team, who were initially informed that the L-11 gun would be used. Predictably, this threw a proverbial spanner into his works. Despite an angry letter to Pavlov demanding blueprints of the gun and at least one sample, there was nothing that could be done: even though the F-32 gun was recommended for service and deemed superior to the L-11 back in the spring of 1939, production was not organized by the end of the year. The L-11 had to be used, if only because it was the only 76.2-mm gun with the requisite ballistics available at the time, and could be installed easily into the L-10 gun mount, meaning that significant changes to the turret were not required. However, the schedule was tight even with the L-11: Kirov factory only prepared two guns for shipment to Kharkov on December 28. This was little consolation, as while the guns were still en route, it turned out that the factory only packed the recoil brake and trigger mechanisms. In order for the weapons to function, factory #183 would still need an elevation mechanism, a brass catcher, a travel lock, the gun mantlet and a clinometer. Maksarev petitioned Pavlov to supply these components on January 19, already past the government's deadline, but the request was not met.

The end was in sight by January 20, 1940, a full five days after the tanks were supposed to be delivered for trials. The factory's military representative reported that the tanks would be ready for breaking-in on January 24/25, and even then it would have to be done without the gun or a number of other components. This prediction turned out to be correct. The first A-34 went out of the factory for its first breaking-in run without observation devices, ammunition racks, instruments or most of the parts of the gun. Breaking-in was completed on February 6, and the tank was presented for military trials on February 10. The second prototype was presented on February 12.[49]

While the engineers were fighting their battle on the manufacturing front, factory management won theirs on the bureaucratic front. Endless lobbying by Maksarev, Koshkin and factory

ABOVE: An A-34 tank after driving through a wire obstacle. Such obstacles would be commonly encountered on a real battlefield, and the tank had to be tested against them thoroughly. *RGVA*

#183's chief engineer Sergei Nestorovich Makhonin paid off. Initially, due to the factory's experience with convertible drive tanks, the plan was to task it with producing the less future-proof and more complicated A-20 tank, while either STZ or factory #174 in Leningrad would produce the A-32. After months of work, factory management convinced first Pavlov, then Likhachev, then ultimately Stalin himself, that the A-32

ABOVE: The same tank photographed from the other side. *RGVA*

Designing the T-34

had more potential. The successful trials of the A-32 that proved its armour could be increased to a thickness of 45 mm were a major victory. As a result, the NKSM decided to cancel the A-20. On November 20, 1939, a draft decree was composed that excluded the A-20 from production and assigned the bulk of the order for A-32 tanks to factory #183.[50]

On December 19, 1939, the Committee of Defence within the Council of Commissars of the USSR signed decree #443ss, defining the Red Army's new armament system and production plans for 1940. Even though the first A-34 was still a pile of parts and an empty hull, this day is commonly considered the birthday of the T-34 tank.

Based on the demonstration and results of trials of new types of tanks, armoured cars, and tractors, produced in accordance with decree #118ss issued by the Committee of Defence on May 15, 1939, the Committee of Defence within the Council of Commissars of the USSR decrees that:

1. The following will be accepted into service with the Red Army:

II: T-32 tank: tracked, with V-2 engine, produced at factory #183, with the following changes:
1. Increase the thickness of main armour plates to 45 mm.
2. Improve visibility from the tank.

ABOVE: A close-up of the wire net wrapped around the tank's tracks. Smaller tanks with weaker engines such as the T-26 would have been immobilized by this kind of obstacle. *RGVA*

ABOVE: The A-34 is not stopped by the wire. The tank keeps driving in third gear and the wire falls out harmlessly. *RGVA*

3. Install the following armament into the T-32 tank:
   a. F-32 76-mm gun with a coaxial 7.62-mm machine gun.
   b. Separate 7.62-mm machine gun for the radio operator.
   c. Separate 7.62-mm machine gun.
   d. 7.62-mm AA machine gun.
   Name this tank 'T-34'.

For factory #183:
1. Organize production of T-34 tanks at the Comintern factory #183 in Kharkov.
2. Produce two experimental T-34 tanks by January 15, 1940, and a pilot batch of 10 tanks by September 15, 1940.
3. Produce no fewer than 200 T-34 tanks in 1940.
4. Increase the factory's annual output to 1,600 T-34 tanks by January 1, 1941.
5. Until full-scale production of T-34 tanks is achieved, continue production of BT tanks with V-2 diesel engines started on December 1, 1939.
6. Produce at least 1,000 BT tanks with V-2 diesel engines in 1940.
7. Remove the BT tank with the V-2 diesel engine from production by 1942, replacing it entirely with the T-34.
8. Starting on February 1, 1940, begin production of the Voroshilovets tractor, producing 600 units in 1940.
9. Starting on January 1, 1940, remove the KIN tractor from production, retaining production of spare parts until it is taken over by other factories.

For STZ:
1. Organize annual output of 2,000 tanks at STZ.
2. Produce 20 T-34 tanks in 1940.
3. Prepare STZ to produce 1,000 T-34 tanks in 1941.
4. Cease preparations for production of the T-26 at STZ.[51]

Even though the initial idea was to only thicken the armour of the A-32, the A-34 ended up a significantly different tank. The army intended to put the two prototypes through their paces in order to find out if the new tanks still satisfied their requirements. On January 23, 1940, Komandarm (Army Commander) 1st Class Grigoriy Ivanovich Kulik signed directive #135669s, defining the trials set for the tanks. Like the A-20 and A-32 before them, they had a 2,500-km-long course to navigate: 300 on paved roads, 1,000 on dirt roads and

Designing the T-34

1,200 off-road. Another 500 km was saved for breaking-in runs at the factory. Due to the late delivery of the tanks, this part of the plan was significantly cut down: A-34 #1 (serial number 311-11-3) was broken in over an 82-km run and A-34 #2 (serial number 311-18-3) was not broken in at all.

Trials of tank #1 began on February 13, 1940. Tank #1 successfully completed a 99-km cross-country drive through snowbanks up to one metre deep. A similar run, 101 km long, was completed on the next day, but an accident occurred at the end of it: the tank drifted on ice and smashed its drive wheel into a concrete post, requiring its replacement. The tank was back in action on February 18, this time driving for 78 km before that day's trials were cut short by an engine malfunction. Tank #2 made its first outing on this day on a 68-km drive.

On February 20, installation of the long-awaited L-11 guns was finally completed. At this moment, the turret traverse was tested. When the tank was standing level, it took 3.5–4.5 kg of effort on the hand-cranked traverse mechanism to rotate the turret, which gave it a relatively high traverse speed: 2–3 rpm. At a tilt of 10 degrees, the amount of effort increased to 28 kg and to 45 kg at 20 degrees. The electric traverse could turn the turret at a speed of 8 rpm when the tank was level and 4.3 rpm when the tank was tilted at 8 degrees. At a tilt of 16 degrees, the turret could still traverse, but the motor struggled.[52]

On February 21, tank #1 made a 17-km run to test the mounting of a new engine. On the next day, both tanks made a 40-km drive to a shooting range to test the L-11 guns. The maximum elevation of the gun

ABOVE: An A-34 tank navigates a ravine muddied by melted snow. The tank's high mobility was a very desirable feature. *RGVA*

was measured to be 24.5 degrees, and the maximum depression was 2.5 degrees. The maximum depression with the gun over the engine deck was only 1.5 degrees, and firing the gun at this angle damaged the protective mesh over the air intake louvres. At these angles of depression, the gun could hit the ground with canister shot at a minimum range of 6 and 11 metres respectively. The aimed rate of fire was only four rounds per minute, due to the difficulty of working in the cramped turret. Firing at a 6x6-metre target at a range of 1,000 metres showed mean deviation of 50 cm horizontally and 30 cm vertically. Even at this stage of the trials, there was already feedback for the designers. The military testers found very little that was satisfactory about the gun except the mount that it was installed on. It was necessary to increase the vertical range of

ABOVE: MB-20 electric motor used to traverse the turret on a number of Soviet tanks, including the T-34. *(SA-Kuva)*

BELOW: An A-34 tank breaks an 879-mm-thick pine tree while driving in third gear. The ability to drive through a thick forest at high speed allowed the tank to appear in places where the enemy did not expect it. *RGVA*

ABOVE: An A-34 tank breaks down a 457-mm-thick pine tree in second gear. The observation port built into the driver's cabin is open. *RGVA*

the gun to -5–+30 degrees, widen the turret to make the gun easier to service, and alter the mesh design to protect it from the blast of the tank's own gun. The position of the telescopic and periscopic sights had to be changed to move the eyepieces to one plane in order to make it easier for the gunner to switch between the two. The reserve ammunition racks also had to be changed to make them easier to access in order to refill the ready racks. Ventilation also had to be improved. Firing the gun rapidly filled the fighting compartment with fumes, which were not extracted by the fan at a satisfactory rate.

Trials held on February 23 and March 2 focused on communications equipment, both internal and external. Trials showed that two A-34 tanks equipped with 71-TK-3 radios could maintain uninterrupted and reliable radio contact at a range of 18–20 kilometres, either at a standstill or during motion. The TPU-2 intercom also functioned flawlessly. Two types of whip antennae were tested, the AShT and ASh, by driving under obstacles with the antenna deployed. During these trials, the ASh proved to be more reliable. Despite the successful performance, the ABTU was still unsatisfied. Their issue with the radio was its position: the radio was located in the turret bustle, and was serviced by the commander. The ABTU required the radio to be installed in the hull, near the bow gunner, to free up space in the turret and free the commander of operating the radio in addition to working the gun and commanding the tank. Since the commander was still expected to be able to communicate directly through the radio, the installation of a TPU-3 intercom was necessary, instead of the TPU-2.[53]

On March 3, the A-34 tanks were put through obstacle trials. The tanks proved to be very agile in winter, capable of navigating through 1.8-metre-deep snowbanks and climbing 15–16-degree hills covered by 1.3–1.6 metres of snow with ease. In the meantime, a much more significant challenge was being prepared for the two prototypes: a march to Moscow and back, a distance of some 800 km. March 6–11 was spent preparing the tanks for this journey. A Voroshilovets tractor, another new design produced by factory #183, was sent along with the tanks carrying spare parts, as delivery from the factory would be complicated. In order to carry as little as possible, parts that were already heavily worn by the trials were replaced. The engines, which were proving themselves to be the weakest link in the design from the point of view of reliability, were replaced in both tanks. One had worked for 71 hours and 47 minutes, the other 76 hours and 26 minutes. This was short of what the V-2 engine achieved in trials of the A-32, and not quite expending the 100-hour warranty period, but it was better to be safe than sorry when preparing for such a long journey.

The column of vehicles left factory #183 on March 12, 1940, at 1600. The weather conditions were not in the tanks' favour, as the highway they were driving on was covered in up to half a metre of snow. Maintenance halts took longer than expected. Koshkin, who was personally accompanying the tanks during their journey, had to return to the factory to attend a meeting on March 14. The rest of the trip took place without him. However, another high-ranking guest, A. A. Goreglyad, joined the convoy when it

ABOVE: A dense forest sometimes means that the tank has to knock down several trees at a time. Here, an A-34 tank knocks down a group of 200–300-mm-thick oak trees. *RGVA*

Designing the T-34

ABOVE: An A-34 tank navigating through a deep snowbank. The wide tracks and powerful engine allowed these tanks to effortlessly smash through defensive barricades made of snow and ice, let alone traverse ordinary snowbanks. *RGVA*

reached Serphukhov. The tanks arrived at factory #37 in Moscow on March 17, at 1645, more than a day behind schedule. With the resources available at the factory, the tanks could undergo more thorough maintenance.

While the tanks were in Moscow, another change was introduced into the trials. Initially, the plan was to simply drive to Moscow and back, but the proximity to the proving grounds at Kubinka made this a good opportunity to test the tank's armour. The tanks were driven from the factory grounds to the shooting range at the NIBT proving grounds near the Kubinka railway station on March 24, 1940. A-34 #1 was chosen as the target for two guns, a 37-mm Bofors gun taken from a captured Finnish Vickers Mark E tank, and a 45-mm 20-K gun from a BT-7 tank. A dummy was placed into the commander's seat to see what damage would be caused by back spall, and the engine was left idling to see if it would stall when the tank was hit. The guns fired two shots each.

Shot #1 was fired by the 37-mm gun into the side of the turret. This shot did not penetrate the armour, leaving only a 17-mm-deep dent, but damaged the observation device. No damage was found on the commander's dummy, nor did the engine stall. The second 37-mm shot was fired into the sloped side armour. It bounced off harmlessly, leaving a 12-mm-deep dent.

The third shot was performed with the 45-mm gun. This time, the gunner targeted a weak point in the armour, the joint between the floor of the turret bustle and the side of the turret. The shell hit the joint, ricocheted and bounced into the turret ring. The result was a lot more significant than in the two shots

Profiles

ABOVE: 4-T-34 1940 profile view. *Thierry Vallet*

ABOVE: 5-T-34 1941 profile view. *Thierry Vallet*

Designing the T-34

ABOVE: T-34 1941 front view. *Thierry Vallet*

ABOVE: T-34 1941 plan view. *Thierry Vallet*

Profiles

ABOVE: T-34 A-20 prototype profile view. *Thierry Vallet*

ABOVE: T-34 A-32#1 profile view. *Thierry Vallet*

Designing the T-34

Profiles

ABOVE: T-34 A-32#2 profile view. *Thierry Vallet*

ABOVE: T-34 A-34 profile view. *Thierry Vallet*

it: the turret jammed, the right observation device was shattered and the weld seam burst. No fragments of the shell penetrated inside the tank, but three strikes were detected on the commander's dummy, as well as a piece of armour that was dislodged by the attack. The fourth shot was fired at the side of the turret, where it did slightly more damage than the 37-mm gun, leaving a 14-mm-deep dent with a bulge on the opposite side. No other damage was caused to the tank. This performance was considered satisfactory. The trials showed that the main armour plates were

ABOVE: An A-34 knocks down a group of pine trees 255–416 mm thick. *RGVA*

ABOVE: Like the A-20, the A-34 was covered in gasoline and set on fire in order to test the degree of protection offered by airtight seals and engine louvres. *RGVA*

sufficiently tough to withstand 37–45-mm cannon fire, but that additional protection of the turret ring and floor of the turret bustle was required. Mobility trials held later that day showed that the gunfire had no effect on the tank's performance.

The results of these trials were incredibly encouraging. On March 29, 1940, an order was jointly signed by the chief of the GlavSpetsMash (Main Directorate of Special Machine Building) G. S. Surenyan and Pavlov to begin preparations for mass production of the A-34 immediately. The tanks were then shown to high-ranking members of government: on March 30 they were shown to Stalin, Kalinin and Voroshilov, and then to NKO and NSKM delegates on March 31. A meeting was held between Voroshilov, Kulik, Pavlov,

LEFT: The A-32 tank was built to withstand 12.7-mm bullets, but its successor carried enough armour to resist fire from anti-tank cannons commonly in use at the time. Impacts from 37-mm and 45-mm armour-piercing shells resulted in negligible damage to the tank's armour. Only the 45-mm shell that hit the underside of the turret bustle ended up breaking the weld seam. *RGVA*

Likhachev, Goreglyad and Koshkin later that day. They summarized the experience of the previous two months of trials and came to the following conclusions:

The T-34 tank, produced to requirements given by the Committee of Defence within the Council of Commissars of the USSR #433ss issued on December 19, 1939, completed government trials and the march from Kharkov to Moscow without any breakdowns or significant defects, and is recommended for immediate production at factory #183 and STZ.

During mass production, consider it necessary to increase the space inside the turret to ensure more comfortable placement of the commander and loader. Increase the space without changing the slopes of the turret armour, hull of the tank, or the turret ring. Place the radio outside of the turret.

Ask the government tank-testing commission to approve blueprints of the T-34 tank for production in 1940 within five days.[54]

At 0130 on April 2, 1940, the two tanks began their triumphant return to Kharkov to finish their trials. The tanks and their accompanying tractor returned to the factory at 0900 on April 10. However, not all was cause for celebration. Early at the start of the drive, the tank Koshkin was riding in slipped and fell into a river. Upon his return to the factory, Koshkin collapsed. A medical examination revealed that he caught pneumonia and needed an operation on a lung abscess. The doctor's efforts were in vain, and on September 26, 1940, Mikhail Ilyich Koshkin died.[55]

ABOVE: Another trial by fire, this time aimed at the front of the tank. *RGVA*

Designing the T-34

Chapter **4**

From A to T

"The T34 with its good armour, ideal shape, and magnificent 76.2-mm long-barrelled cannon was universally feared and a threat to every German tank up until the end of the war."

Otto Carius, Tigers in the Mud

ABOVE: A pilot T-34 at the proving grounds. The tanks were often submitted for trials before assembly was completely finished in order to meet tight deadlines. In this case, headlights are not yet installed. The front of the tank is labelled 'front section', likely a marking left over from the assembly process. *RGVA*

The T-34 may have been accepted into service, but it was too early for design bureau #520 to rest on its laurels. Like with any prototype, the trials of the A-34 revealed a number of drawbacks that would have to be corrected before it entered mass production. A commission met at factory #183 on April 20/21, 1940, to discuss a number of design changes what would have to be made to the T-34 tank. The list of changes requested was rather lengthy, 105 in all. These changes were approved on April 27. Morozov, who replaced Koshkin as the factory's chief designer, had a lot to do.

Specifically, trials showed that maintenance of the tank took a lot longer than anticipated. One of the main reasons why the drive from Kharkov to Moscow and back fell behind schedule was that even trivial tasks such as filling up the tank with fuel and oil were time consuming. Lubrication points had to be moved and various components made easier to access. It was at this stage that the hinged transmission access plate, one of the distinguishing features of the T-34's design, was suggested. A maintenance manual also needed to be written.

The pneumatic servo controls that made the tank so easy to drive (the amount of effort required to turn the tank was no greater than 7 kg) were also unsatisfactory. Pneumatic servos were complicated and difficult to service, and would have to be replaced with mechanical servos in production. Aside from the servos, the driver's station was deemed satisfactory and comfortable (provided the driver was under 175 cm in height), but the driver had no easy means of exiting the tank other than the turret hatch. Another distinguishing feature of the T-34, the driver's hatch in the front plate, was suggested here.

BELOW: The same tank from behind. The transmission access hatch is labelled 'rear section'. This photograph shows that the weak spot in the engine louvre cover on the A-34 was no longer present on the T-34. *RGVA*

Designing the T-34

ABOVE: This angle shows all of the features of an early T-34: the driver's hatch with one observation device and no splash-proofing, narrow-type turret with the radio installed in the turret bustle, L-11 gun, and upper and lower front hull made from one curved plate. The cover above the engine louvres is missing. An assembly marking is also visible on the right side of the hull. *RGVA*

The radio operator's station was criticized more harshly. Minor changes, like adjusting the seat, would be easy to make. The ABTU's chief concern was that the radio was in the turret, instead of the hull. The radio operator could not actually operate it in this state, and effectively served as just a hull gunner.

The position of the radio came up in criticism of the commander's station as well. In addition to the aforementioned drawbacks in the positions of the sights, his seat was deemed loose, position of the trigger pedal too close to the seat, plus the space between the side of the turret and brass catcher was only 450 mm, slightly narrower than an average person's shoulder span. The loader's position was similarly criticized, with the additional comment that there were no machine-gun magazines available in the turret, which reduced the effective rate of fire, since the loader had to bend down to retrieve the ammunition.

In addition to correcting these specific drawbacks, it was ordered that the tank should have a thermos for food and water, a place to store the crew's personal belongings and equipment, and padding and handholds to prevent the crew from injury while driving on bumpy terrain. New observation devices for all crew members were also required, with the ability to clear them from condensation, mud and snow without getting out of the tank. The observation devices had to be resistant to impact from shell fragments and bullets.

The reliability of the engine was also insufficient for the commission. It was ruled that the warranty period of the V-2 should be raised from 100 to 250 hours with minimum loss of power towards the end of this period. The air filter was deemed satisfactory, but it was hard to remove and install due to its size. A new cooling fan was requested, as the existing design failed several times during the trials. Resolution to the issues with warping of friction disks in the main clutch after prolonged use in difficult road conditions was also requested. The commission ordered additional summertime trials to test the effectiveness of the engine and air filter in more demanding conditions.

There were also additional suggestions from the Artillery Committee. Military Engineer 2nd Class R. E. Sorokin, who was present at the meeting, suggested that, in addition to widening the turret, it should be made about 60 mm taller. The resulting decrease in the side plates (from 30 to 28 degrees) would not make much of a difference from the point of view of protection, but this change would allow the tank to use the gun mount developed at the Kirov factory for the KV-1 tank, as well as improve the maximum gun depression. However, this suggestion was ultimately declined.

BELOW: A V-2 diesel engine recovered from a T-34 tank. Work on diesel engines began in the USSR in the early 1930s. The BD-2 engine was successfully tested and installed in a BT-5 tank in 1933. The V-2 evolved from that design, and descendants of this engine family are still in production to this day. *T-34 Tank Museum*

This was not the only part of the original proposal that was scrapped. Morozov contested a number of findings of the government commission:

ABOVE: The original narrow turret used on the A-34 and early T-34 tanks. Trials showed that it was not roomy enough to fit a crew of two in addition to the 76-mm gun. Only 38 of these turrets were built. *RGVA*

On the 'Radio' section: the existing 71-TK-3 radio cannot be moved to the bow of the tank, both due to the dimensions and the requirements for installation of the radio. The Communications Directorate of the Red Army has the same opinion. Installation in the bow will also require a new intercom, which is not available at this time, and the development of an antenna mount in the sloped hull armour.

Given these and other drawbacks of this type of installation, it will not be possible to move the 71-TK-3 radio to the bow.

On the 'Observation devices' section: the factory cannot propose any other type of observation devices at the moment. The commission's comment regarding development of new devices is

ABOVE: The same turret from the left side. From this angle one can see that the periscope port and pistol port are dead centre in the side of the turret. These features would be slightly forward from the centre of the curve on later widened turrets. *RGVA*

ABOVE: Fragment of a widened turret and other T-34 parts recovered near Moscow. The remnants of the welding seam that held on the appliqué armour can be seen. The observation periscope housing was cast separately from the turret armour and then welded on.
T-34 Tank Museum

accepted, but a final conclusion can only be given after the production of these devices and trials in a vehicle.

On the '360-degree observation device' section: the 360-degree observation device might not provide full traverse, but as it is an auxiliary observation device, it is generally satisfactory. Since the commission did not list any deficiencies of the device other than stating that it is unfit, and the factory has no other type of device, we cannot provide any replacement for the 1940 production year.

On section XVI: the commission's statements regarding the widening of the turret are not specific. Without changing the turret ring, hull, and turret armour slope, the turret can be widened by only 160 mm. Further changes are only possible by changing the turret ring, hull, and the turret itself.[56]

Pavlov was forced to give in on some level. In addition to giving an exemption from these demands to the first ten tanks, he agreed to leave the 360-degree periscope, but insisted on new observation devices, moving the radio and widening the turret without increasing its height.

All of these suggestions were compiled into a single report, which was sent up the chain of command for approval. On May 31, 1940, Semyon Konstantinovich Timoshenko, Voroshilov's replacement as the People's Commissar of Defence, approved these changes.[57]

Interestingly enough, even though a widened turret was designed and approved by the ABTU, the first draft never entered production. The tools available at the Mariupol factory were simply incapable

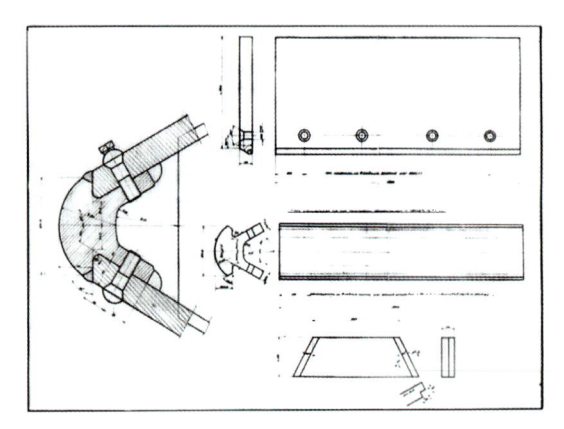

ABOVE: Diagram of the cast beam connecting upper and lower front plates. The 100-mm-thick beam offered better protection than the curved single piece front hull and also made the hull of the T-34 easier to produce. *RGVA*

of producing this design, and a different design had to be developed that could be built more easily using existing equipment. A second meeting regarding the turrets was held on June 12, where the new simplified turret was accepted for production by the Mariupol factory. The fighting compartment became 160 mm wider, which gave the commander and loader some much-needed breathing room. These turrets can be distinguished by a rectangle of appliqué armour welded below and in front of the pistol port on each side. The majority of T-34 tanks with welded turrets received a widened turret. Only 38 narrow turrets were built. The improved turrets were assembled at factory #183 starting in August of 1940.

Another important decision was made at this meeting regarding the armour of the T-34. Originally, the T-34's front hull armour was made from one rolled plate, which was bent to form the pointed bow. Not only was rolling such a large piece of armour and then bending it a complicated operation, but the end result had a weak zone, as the very front of the tank was still 45 mm thick, but not presented at a slope to increase the effectiveness of this protection. A solution was developed to solve both of these problems. The upper and lower front plates would be produced separately. A cast beam, 100 mm thick, was used to connect them together, giving this part of the hull equivalent protection to the upper and lower front plates.[58] The composite front hull was tested at Mariupol factory in May–June of 1940. A series of shots aimed at both the beam and the plates failed to break the rivet-reinforced weld seams that joined the beam to the upper and lower front plates. As a result, the composite hull was accepted into production in June. A fully cast front hull was also designed, but never produced.[59] The new hull entered production slightly sooner than the new turret, and a small number of tanks ended up with the new hull, but the old narrower turret.

Pavlov's exemption for the first ten tanks was quite fortunate, as production of these tanks had already started by the time changes were requested. The parts to assemble the first two tanks were almost completely finished by May 15, 1940. A number of assemblies for installation into the first tank were also completed.[60] While the tanks were being assembled, the changes recommended by the ABTU were being put through their paces on the prototype A-34 tanks. Trials of the mechanical servo device were completed on the same day. The ABTU commission concluded that the new design was satisfactory: it made the tank easy to drive, did not cause the driver to become tired after prolonged operation and did not require special or complicated maintenance.[61] These trials also tested a new type of track links which were cast rather than stamped. These tracks were used over the course of 417 km of harsh trials, including driving on cobblestones and braking at full speed, and performed admirably. Pilot-batch T-34s and all production tanks received these types of tracks until the end of 1940,[62] despite never actually receiving approval from the ABTU.[63] Even though these track links were easier to produce, the tracks had a lifespan of only 1,000 km,[64] a far cry from the 2,000-km reliability requirement.[65]

The pilot tanks were already somewhat different from the A-34. The driver's cabin provided on the prototypes offered excellent vision for the driver, but was a fairly large weak point. The hatch in the top of the cabin could not be opened if the turret was blocking it. To resolve this, a new type of hatch was made that was flush with the upper front plate of the tank. One observation device was installed in the hatch itself, and two more in slots to the left and to the right of it.

ABOVE: Trials showed that the connection between the upper and lower front plates and the connecting beam did not break apart, even under extremely heavy attack from 45-mm and 76-mm guns. *RGVA*

ABOVE: The opposite side of the test assembly, showing the design of the connecting beam. Three shots (one 76 mm, two 45 mm) penetrated the 45-mm armour at normal range, but none penetrated the cast beam. Localized cracking of the weld seam from shots ##4, 6 and 8 is outlined in chalk.

The rear armour changed as well. Vulnerabilities caused by the location of the engine louvre cover were corrected, and the joint between the rear plate and the bottom of the hull was also changed to eliminate a weak point. A number of the armour plates were also thickened: the upper and lower rear plates from 35 to 40 mm, the front of the floor from 15 to 16 mm, the front of the roof from 15 to 20 mm and the engine compartment roof from 10 to 16 mm.[66]

As early as June, the T-34 chassis was already a candidate for development of other vehicles. Three tanks (two in June and one in July) were sent to factory #8 for development of an 85-mm-gun-armed tank destroyer. A project of a tractor on the T-34 chassis was completed at factory #183 in August.

Requests for changes continued to come in, be debated and either discarded or slotted into the production schedule. On July 26, 1940, a list of 55 changes was agreed upon between factory #183 and the ABTU. Some of these changes were important enough to be installed into all T-34 tanks, including those already being assembled, such as improving the turret traverse controls and observation device clips. Others, such as adding stowage brackets for tools and equipment and changes to make maintenance operations easier, would only be introduced starting with tank #11, after the completion of the pilot batch. Others were scheduled even further down the production line, postponed until 1941, or not scheduled at all, as it was impossible to say when development of the solution would be completed.[67] Requests to solve specific and immediate issues were combined with long-term modernization and improvement work to create a research and development plan for 1941. This plan was approved on August 1, 1940, and included work on warming the tank in the winter, improving the firepower of the tank, improving the turret traverse mechanism to be able to work at any angle of tilt, placement of the radio into the hull and installation of a flamethrower. Other suggestions were more radical: moving from rolled to cast armour (especially for the turret), changing the shape of the hull to make it more ballistically resistant and simpler to produce, and development of a torsion bar suspension.[68]

The use of cast components was not a new idea. Casting the turret was an economically effective move. Calculations at the Mariupol factory showed that production of one set of armour cost 60 hours of using high-power presses, which would not allow the factory to produce the armour in sufficient volumes. A group of engineers was sent from the NII-48 research institute to develop a cast turret. The ABTU was fine with this change, assuming that the resistance of the armour was maintained and the new turret did not overload the chassis. The engineers' work was difficult, as the USSR had never cast highly hardened armour before. The only significant armoured castings to this point were made from low hardness armour. Work on a cast T-34 turret started back in January 1940, as it would take a very long time to select the proper type of steel and develop a manufacturing process. Trials of steel already used in production showed that MZ-2 was still the best kind of steel for the job. Design of a new cast turret began in the second half of March 1940. The first experimental turret was ready in April. Trials of the turret showed defects in the casting, but the results were promising. After reviewing the results of the trials, the engineers made a number of changes. The shape of the turret was simplified and its curves smoothed, which made the casting process easier. A pilot batch of 13 turrets was produced for trials in early June. Trials of this batch were performed on July 4. In total, 32 shots were fired into

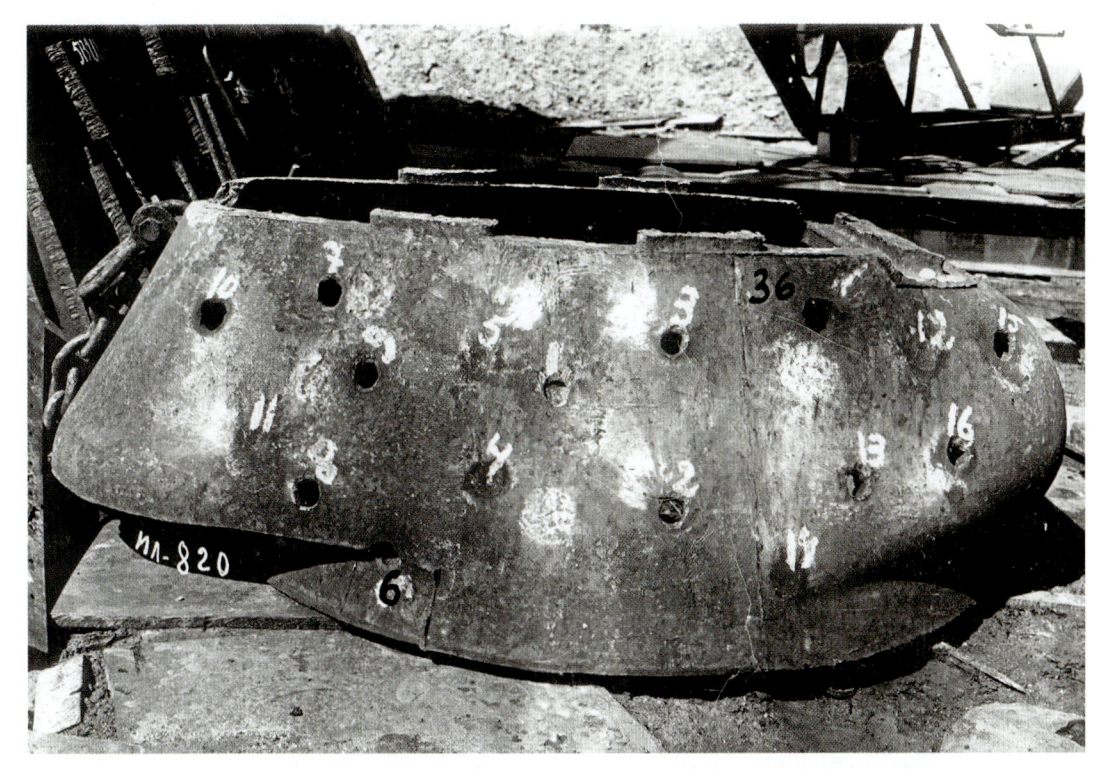

ABOVE: A prototype cast turret after ballistics trials. New armoured components were put through harsh testing in order to ensure that they offered sufficient protection under heavy attack. *RGVA*

ABOVE: The same turret from the other side. *RGVA*

Designing the T-34

the turrets with 37-, 45- and 76-mm guns. The results were fully satisfactory. The trials commission remarked that the armour did not spall or crack even when hit with 76-mm rounds. The complete penetration ballistic limit of the 45-mm blunt-tipped armour-piercing shell against this armour was 760 m/s. In other words, the gun would have to be right up against the armour plate in order to stand a chance of penetration. The sharp-tipped armour-piercing shell could penetrate the side of the turret from

ABOVE: Trials of a pilot turret. This turret has the casing for the observation device as a part of the main casting. On later models these casings were cast separately and welded into place. *RGVA*

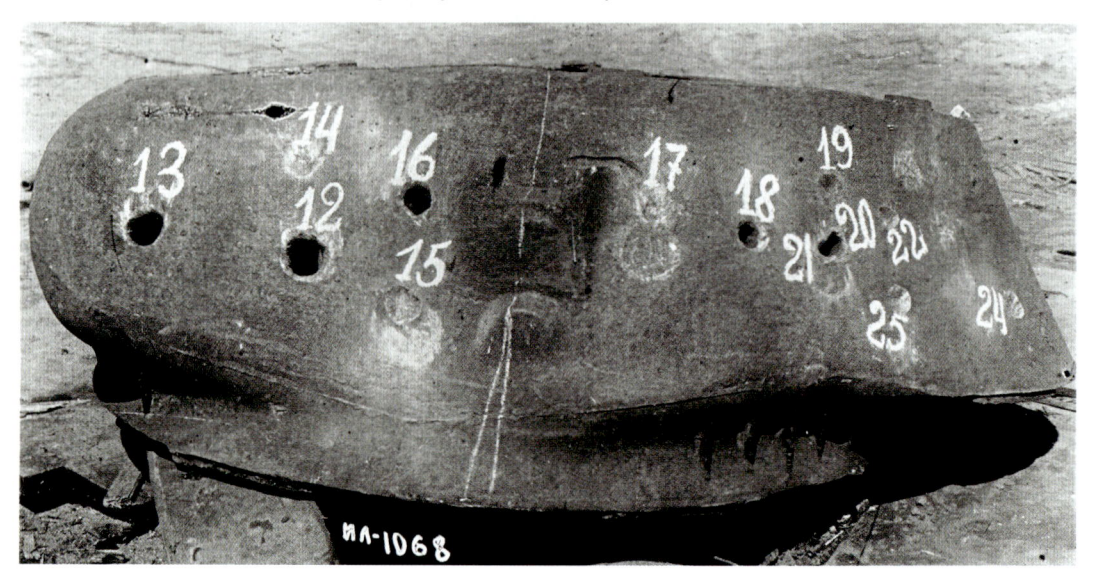

ABOVE: The pilot turret from the other side. *RGVA*

100 metres. Cast armour to a 51–55 mm thickness was fully equivalent to the resistance provided by 45 mm of rolled armour. This increased thickness came at a cost: a cast turret weighed 2,035 kg, noticeably heavier than a welded turret's weight of 1,885 kg.[69]

In late July, a report on the results of the trials and draft technical requirements were sent to Moscow for approval. The ABTU immediately gave its permission. The first production batch of cast turrets arrived at factory #183 in late August. The Committee of Defence accepted the cast turret and composite hull into service on October 9, 1940.[70] These turrets were installed on tanks starting in November/December 1940.[71]

Another meeting was held on August 29, this time to discuss the armament. As mentioned earlier, the F-32 gun was chosen for the T-34, but mass production of this gun had still not been set up in time. The GAU could only provide 200 L-11 76.2-mm guns for T-34 production in 1940. Any tanks produced past that number that would have to be armed with 45-mm guns. Since there was still no F-32 gun mount for the T-34, one would have to be designed by November 10, 1940. The same gun mount would be used on the KV-1, since unification between the two types was desirable, but the mount from the KV-1 did not fit into the T-34's turret. The mantlet-mounted spotlight was removed, since the ABTU decided to drop this requirement from all tanks in production. In addition to these changes, a list of 30 items was agreed upon between Maksarev and Fedorenko, detailing design defects and omissions that would have to be resolved before the end of 1940.[72]

The position of the radio in the T-34 tank had been a point of contention between the ABTU and factory #183 since the original A-34 design. On one hand, placing the radio in the turret inconvenienced both the loader and the gunner/commander. The loader had no machine-gun ammunition quickly accessible to him, and the commander had to work the radio in addition to firing the gun and observing the battlefield. On the other hand, it was simply impossible to fit the radio into the hull, as the 71-TK-3 radio set was too large. A potential solution was examined on April 9, 1940. This layout left much to be desired, as the receiver was difficult to adjust, the radio components got in the way of regular service of the tank and the antenna went through an opening in the upper front plate, weakening the armour severely.[73] The rejection of this proposal reignited the debate on whether or not the radio could be installed into the hull at all. Since no acceptable solution could be found in time, the T-34 was put into production as is, and the location of the radio would be switched as soon as a solution was available, at the cost to factory #183.[74]

Work on a new radio layout began on July 11, 1940. The designers' job was made slightly easier on July 17, when the requirement for installation of the TK-12 encryption device was dropped. The work was done by August 12. This time, the radio antenna was installed in a rotating mount on the right side of the hull. If the antenna was hit by the gun or turret during rotation, it would fold down automatically. It could also be folded down manually from inside the tank. Three different types of antenna mounts were designed. Trials would show which one was the most suitable.

Trials of the resulting layout of radio components showed that improvements were still necessary. A number of radios shipped to the factory also did not account for the increased antenna length and did not support a range of required frequencies. The position of the receiver was still awkward, and the operator had to lean down to adjust the dials, a complicated

Designing the T-34

operation when the tank was in motion, to say the least. Nevertheless, the GABTU (the reformed ABTU) got what they asked for: a radio operator who could actually operate the radio. A number of improvements were suggested as a result of the trials.[75] In addition to those, another change was made: an experimental TPU-3M intercom was installed on the tank with serial number 0618-4. This intercom allowed the commander of the tank to communicate with the driver and the radio operator, as well as talk through the radio directly without having to pass orders to the operator. This tank (referred to as tank #2 in the trials) also received an improved version of the equipment layout, incorporating suggestions made by the GABTU. Tank 0618-3 (tank #1 in the trials report) had the old TPU-2 intercom and original layout. These tanks were used to test the effectiveness

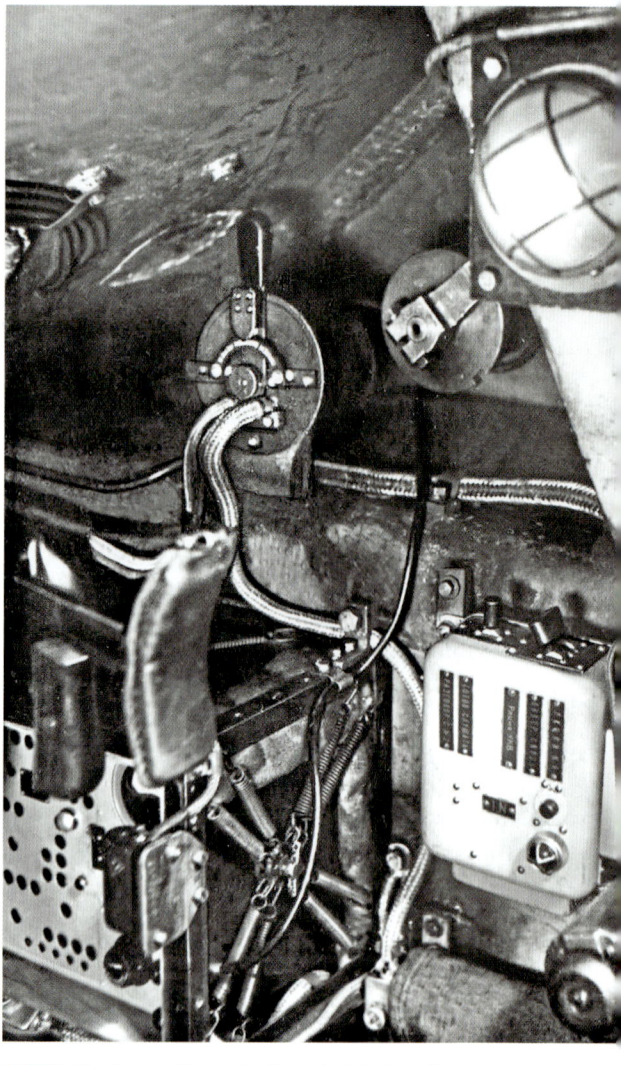

ABOVE: The transmitter and other electrical equipment were installed to the right of the radio operator. *RGVA*

ABOVE LEFT: One of the main complaints about the T-34 tank was that the radio was installed in the turret, and not the hull, Even though it was initially considered impossible to fit the 71-TK-3 radio in the hull of the tank in a satisfactory manner, a number of layouts were tried, and the third was deemed satisfactory. The radio receiver was installed in front of the radio operator, below the machine gun. *RGVA*

of radio communication with the new layout on September 19, 1940. With both tanks at a standstill, communication could be maintained at a range of 18–20 km (greater range was not tested). With tank #1 standing still and tank #2 driving at a speed of 30–35 kph over rough terrain, communications could be maintained at a range of 10–12 km before interference from nearby wireless stations made communications impossible. These trials showed that tank #2 was superior: the TPU-3M intercom allowed the commander to communicate through the radio as clearly as his radio operator could, and the layout made it easier to service the receiver and transmitter both in motion and while stopped. This solution was still not perfect, and a new layout was proposed by the GABTU commission on September 22. Instead of being installed on top of one another, this layout had the transmitter to the right of the operator, between the suspension springs, and the receiver in front of him. This layout was implemented in both tanks 0618-3 and 0618-4 on September 28, along with other improvements. These changes had positive results: range increased to up to 15–16 km with both tanks in motion and 25–26 with both tanks stationary.[76]

Another round of changes was suggested, which took longer to implement. Two new experimental tanks, #608-01 and #547-29, were equipped with 71-TK-3 radios and new TPU-3M intercoms were finished on October 12. Trials held on October 12 revealed that bidirectional communication could be reliably maintained between two tanks driving in third or fourth gear at a range of 17–18 km. A fifth T-34 tank with a radio in the hull, number 423-41, joined them on October 14, and demonstrated reliable voice communication at a range of 18–19 km.[77] The long-running drama of equipping the T-34 with a radio was finally over. The factory began delivering its first tanks with the radio installed in the hull in October 1940. Only seven production tanks with the radio in the turret were built. These tanks were sent to training facilities and factories as samples, so they do not often appear in photographs.[78]

There was another potential solution. The KRSTB radio set was designed at the NII-20 research institute in 1939 and completed laboratory and then factory trials by the end of the year. The radio was perfect for installation into a tank: not only was it significantly smaller than the 71-TK-3, it worked on fixed frequencies, meaning there was no chance that the settings would drift due to shaking of the

ABOVE: The radio antenna base was protected by an armoured cup. Unlike in the initial proposal, where the opening for the antenna was drilled through the front of the hull, it was installed on the right side of the tank where the weakened armour was not as critical. *RGVA*

ABOVE: The T-34 was approved for production with the F-32 76.2-mm gun, but this type of gun was never used due to production issues. Instead, the F-34 76.2-mm gun was installed on T-34 tanks after March 1941. This gun belonged to a T-34 tank sent to Great Britain during World War II. *Bovington Tank Museum*

tank in motion, and that the operator could switch between predefined frequencies with ease instead of fiddling with dials. The communications range was also much greater: when installed in BT-7 and T-26 tanks, two radios could communicate by voice at ranges of 20–25 km in motion and 30–35 km while standing. Communication in telegraph mode could be performed at a range of 40–45 km with a 4-metre antenna.[79] However, there was one weakness of this design: it relied on highly precise quartz disks, which were in short supply in the USSR. The ABTU considered it unlikely that the KRSTB would be available in sufficient numbers to meet demand. Their predictions turned out to be right: the radio was only mass produced for use in tanks in 1942 under the index 10-RT.[80] In the meantime, the only choice was to use the 71-TK-3 radio, although the KRSTB was still tested in two T-34 tanks in February 1941.[81]

The gun was also no longer satisfactory. Despite the great lengths Morozov's team went to install the L-11 gun into the A-34 prototypes, it was only ever going to be acceptable as a temporary measure. The L-11 was more powerful than the L-10 originally used on the A-32, capable of penetrating 50 mm of armour sloped at 30 degrees at 300 metres, or 40 mm sloped at 30 degrees at 900 metres in practical trials.[82] However, the firepower was not the problem. Like the L-10 before it, the L-11 showed issues with the recoil mechanism. These issues did not improve with time: for example, during trials held on November 10, 1940, one L-11 gun failed to return into battery after the second shot, then started jamming after the 39th shot. Another gun tested at the same time functioned normally.[83] Even though the reasons for these faults were found and remedied,[84] these kinds of issues were a reminder that the L-11 was only a temporary solution, and that a replacement had to be found quickly. A meeting was held between representatives of the GABTU, factory #183 and factory #92 on September 8, 1940, to discuss whether or not the new F-34 tank gun could be installed into the turret of a T-34 tank. A promising decision was reached: it would be possible to design a gun mount that was compatible with both the F-32 and F-34 guns, and then seamlessly switch once the new gun became available. Interestingly enough, a note on the document reads that factory #183 was authorized to install 45-mm guns in the meantime, showing just how much the ABTU disliked the L-11.[85] The F-34 was yet another significant step forward in firepower. Its armour-piercing shell penetrated 60 mm of armour at 30 degrees from 400 metres and 50 mm of armour at 30 degrees from 800 metres in trials, making it a lethal anti-tank weapon.[86] A mount for the F-34 gun was developed by the end of 1940. A tank with the experimental gun was tested successfully in November 1940. Production of the tank with the new gun was supposed to start on January 1, 1941. However, there were some delays. The initial design of the gun mantlet was cast (similar to the one used on the L-11) and had a variable thickness of 18–35 mm. This was unsatisfactory for two reasons: one was that the mantlet was weaker than the main turret armour, the other was that it was impossible for Mariupol factory to produce a cast gun mantlet, as they had no casting facilities to spare. A new stamped manlet had to be designed, which took until early February.[87] This delayed production of tanks armed with F-34 guns until March. Two hundred and sixty-eight tanks equipped with the L-11 gun were produced until then, 103 with radios and 165 without.

Another important change to the T-34's firepower was made around this time. Trials of improved ammunition racks had been completed by March 1, 1941. The tank still carried 77 rounds of ammunition, but in a much more convenient way. It took nine to ten minutes to load the tank fully (compared to two to two and a half hours with the old design). Removing the ammunition was also much easier. The tank crew could now sustain an aimed rate of fire of four rounds per minute over prolonged periods of time, or three rounds per minute if firing on the move, including time spent correcting misfires. It was also much easier to remove the ammunition bins to service elements of the tank that they obstructed. This experimental tank also featured new seats for the commander and loader, as well as a prototype driver's hatch with two observation devices, an improved version of which would enter production in August of 1941.[88]

The F-34 gun was not the only firepower upgrade the T-34 received. In the spring of 1941, Soviet intelligence received information about new German 'Type V', 'Type VI' and 'Type VII' heavy tanks. Unlike relatively thinly armoured German medium tanks known to the USSR at the time, these monsters allegedly had well over 100 mm of front armour, which was more than the F-34 could handle. In addition to a tank destroyer project armed with an 85-mm gun in a new turret, another effort was

Designing the T-34

ABOVE: F-34 gun, showing breech and elevation mechanism. *Bovington Tank Museum*

ABOVE: F-34 gun, showing the coaxial machine-gun mount. *Bovington Tank Museum*

RIGHT: Empty 76.2-mm casings and fully assembled rounds: armour-piercing (left) and high-explosive (right). *Patriot Park*

made to improve the T-34's anti-tank capabilities, this time without changing the turret. This solution used a high-velocity 57-mm gun based on the towed ZIS-2 anti-tank gun. The tank version of this weapon was named ZIS-4. Work on installing this gun in the T-34 tank began in early 1941. A prototype was built in April 1941 and tested in May. Trials showed that the gun had impressive penetration (70 mm at a 30-degree angle at a range of 1,000 metres), but had poorer precision compared to the standard F-34 gun and a barrel lifespan of only 900 rounds. Nevertheless, the idea of equipping the T-34 with a high-velocity 57-mm gun was deemed correct. An improved design went through trials from July 6 to July 18, 1941. The improved version of the gun showed satisfactory precision at a range of 2,000 metres.[89] However, it was already clear that the heavily armoured German phantoms weren't coming, and so only a handful of these tanks were ever built. These tanks are often referred to as 'T-34-57' today, but this index was never used. Contemporary official documents refer to it as the 'T-34 with a 57-mm gun', 'T-34 with ZIS-4' and 'T-34 tank destroyer'.[90]

Removable grousers were designed, tested and put into production. Grousers were attached to track links by means of bolts inserted through two holes. A crew of three took two and a half to three hours to install the grousers.[91] The weight of the grousers (30 in total per tank) and the clips that held them while they were not in use was 255 kg.[92]

Another experiment was performed in 1940 that could have significantly changed the T-34: trials of the new M-250 engine. This was a very promising prototype engine. During trials on a test bench held from April 16 to May 8, 1940, the engine worked for 350 hours. Such an impressive result gave the green light for trials in a real tank. These tests were authorized on June 21, 1940. The objective was to run for 250 hours under load, two and a half times as long as the V-2 was expected to last. Two prototype engines were installed in A-34 tanks, one by July 31 and one by August 13. Trials began on August 2, without waiting for the second tank to be converted. By August 22, one M-250 engine was removed from trials due to excessive loss of power. By that point it had worked for 114 hours and 32 minutes, not a large improvement over the V-2. The second engine suffered a breakdown after running for 103 hours. The last M-250 prototype, which had already run for 48 hours on a test bench, was sent as a replacement. The engine broke down after 75 hours and 21 minutes of running in the A-34. A decision was made to stop trials of the M-250, since it clearly fell far short of expectations and did not perform much better than the V-2 did. Several design elements from the M-250 were later used to extend the V-2's service life.[93] Trials held in January 1941 showed that the improved V-2 engine could run for over 150 hours.[94]

Experiments in improving the T-34's armour were also performed. Decree

ABOVE: Ammunition storage, showing two three-round ready racks and bins on the floor. *Private collection*

Designing the T-34

of the Council of People's Commissars and Central Committee of the VKP(b) #1216-502ss, dated May 7, 1941, required factory #183's design bureau to develop 13–15-mm-thick appliqué armour for T-34 tanks. A T-34 tank was loaded to 28.5 tons and run through 1,697 km of trials to determine if this was possible. These trials showed that the T-34's chassis could take the extra weight without impacting reliability, but the implementation of the armour left much to be desired. The 13-mm-thick appliqué armour increased the ballistic limit of penetration by 40–55 m/s, but the plates fell off when hit, since they were held on with bolts. Only two T-34 tanks received this style of additional armour: one with serial number 0618-9 (1940 production, L-11 gun, one piece front hull) and 811-28 (1941 production, F-34 gun, composite hull).[95]

As one can see, early T-34 tanks were in a state of nearly constant flux. New improvements were constantly being developed, produced, tested and either approved or rejected. This process makes it difficult to identify discrete variants of the T-34, and designations invented after the war ('model 1940'/'model 1941' or T-34A/T-34B/T-34C) mean very little when applied to tanks that were produced in real life.

In addition to various experimental work, large trials of three mass-production T-34 tanks were conducted in October–December 1940. Tanks produced in late September to early October were chosen for these trials.

ABOVE: A T-34 tank armed with a 57-mm ZIS-4 gun. The F-34 offered good all-round performance, but the ZIS-2 had higher penetration at the expense of a smaller and less effective high-explosive round. Very few of these specialized tanks were built. TsAMO

ABOVE: A removable grouser, which gave the tank improved mobility in mud or snow. The track link behind it has holes that were used to attach the grouser.
T-34 Tank Museum

The trials were even longer than the ones the two A-34 tanks went through. These three tanks were to drive from Kharkov to Kubinka, then to Smolensk, Kiev and back to Kharkov. Gunnery trials would be performed at each stop in order to evaluate the tank's readiness for combat after a long march. Other aspects of the tank such as communication devices, ease of repair, mobility in difficult terrain and ability to perform in a platoon were also tested.

Since tactical-technical characteristics of the T-34 tank had not yet been established, the trials started with measurements of the tanks. The production T-34 tanks weighed in at 25.2 tons dry and 26.8 tons loaded for combat. During trials, the tanks showed a top highway speed of 54 kph. Average speed was 30.2 kph on a highway and 25 kph on dirt roads. The tanks could cross a 3.4–3.5-metre-wide trench, climb up a 30-degree slope without grousers, climb over a 730-mm-tall wall, cross a 1.3-m-deep river, knock down an individual tree up to 900 mm in diameter, or drive through a dense forest of trees up to 300 mm in diameter. Driving at a tilt of 20 degrees could be confidently performed, and a maximum of 30 degrees could be held for a short period of time, after which the tank began to slip. The effectiveness of the stamped track links with smooth surfaces was judged insufficient. The tank consumed 1.56 litres of fuel per kilometre on a highway and 2 l on a dirt road, which gave it a cruising range of 292 and 227 km respectively. In total, the tanks drove for 2,706, 2,571 and 2,680 km, working for 132 hours and 27 minutes, 120 hours and 35 minutes, and 129 hours respectively. The report concluded that the engines reached the required warranty period of 100 hours, but for such a valuable tank it was desirable to increase it even further to 250 hours.

Trials of the radio showed a maximum range of 20 km for verbal communication while stationary and 15–17 km while driving. However, the range decreased to 7–8 km after driving for 2,600 km due to loosening of the components. The use of the TPU-3M intercom to talk through the radio had no effect on the quality of communication.

Gunnery trials performed after 2,500 km of driving showed that the best 50 per cent of shots fired at 600 metres landed within 30 cm vertical and 52 cm horizontal bounds in tank #1 and 60 cm and 94 cm respectively in tank #3. It was stated that large tolerances in the turret ring and elevation mechanism increased dispersion of the gun. However, it was still better than the nominal performance of the 76-mm mod.1927 gun, which was 1.08 by 1.44 metres. The practical rate of aimed fire on the move as measured in tank #1 was 4.2 rpm (11 shots made in 2 minutes and 35 seconds). While stationary, the crew could achieve a maximum rate of aimed fire of 5–6 rpm. The rate of fire was reduced, in part, due to the fact that the loader's seat was not collapsible and got in his way. Another factor that reduced the rate of fire was the fact that the ventilation system was not sufficiently powerful to deal with the build-up of fumes, even with the engine running.

The visibility from the tank's turret was judged insufficient. It was also hard to use the TOD-6 telescopic sight to aim the gun, but the PT-6 periscopic sight was entirely satisfactory. This sight also offered better all-round vision than the auxiliary rotating periscope installed behind the commander, which could only be used to observe in a 120-degree-wide arc. The observation devices in the sides of the turret helped, but the turret crewmen had to slouch down to look through them.

In comparison, the driver's triple observation devices gave him excellent vision, but they became covered in mud after driving off-road for five to ten minutes. The wiper installed on the central observation device did not work well enough to keep it completely clear. Keeping observation devices clean from

ABOVE: A production T-34 tank before undergoing large-scale trials. The tanks that took part in the November trials already looked different from the pilot tanks. From the front, one can see the riveted connecting beam between the lower and upper front plates. *RGVA*

ABOVE: The tanks had additional fuel tanks installed along each side. The appliqué armour used on the widened turret is also visible. *RGVA*

ABOVE: From this side, one can see the radio antenna in the folded-down position, as well as two more external fuel tanks. *RGVA*

Designing the T-34

mud, dust and precipitation was a big problem in general.

A number of conclusions were made from these trials to improve the tank. In order to place the observation devices and weapons more effectively, the turret would have to be enlarged. The trigger pedal for the gun had to be replaced with a button on the aiming mechanism flywheel handle. The flywheels themselves had to be moved to make them more comfortable to use. To improve the work of the hull gunner, he would have to receive an optical sight for his machine gun and a cover to prevent dirt from entering through the machine-gun ball mount. The TOD-6 telescope used by the gunner was unsatisfactory, and was to be replaced with the improved TMF telescopic sight.

The report was full of complaints about the design and production quality of various parts of the tank. Since the T-34 had barely entered production and was a huge revolutionary leap compared to the tanks that came before it, such growing pains were to be expected. Despite all the drawbacks listed, the report makes a very favourable conclusion:

> The firepower, armour, type and power of engine, and the cruising range of the T-34 dictates that it must become the prevailing tank in the Red Army's system of armament due to the wide range of tactical uses of this tank.[96]

ABOVE: Unlike the relatively bare pilot tanks, these models carried spare track links, removable grousers and toolboxes. The production tank's rear plate was hinged, which allowed easy access to the transmission. *RGVA*

Chapter 5
Production and Service

ABOVE: T-34 tank with the name *Stalinets*, serial number 0517-4. This tank left factory #183 on May 12, 1941, and is the only pre-war production T-34 known to survive to this day. The tank was captured in 1941 and put on a railway platform to be used as a mobile observation post on a firing range.[97] The tank was moved from Germany to Russia in the 1980s. Wheels and tracks currently installed on this tank were taken from a T-34-85.[98] Today, it can be seen on display at Patriot Park, Russia.

> "The T-34 heavy tank is the most dangerous tank in the Red Army... Its effective armament, skilful angling of thick armour, and mobility, make it a very serious opponent."
>
> *Lecture titled 'Tank Units of the Soviet Union', Wunsdorf Tank Academy, March 1, 1942*

While the designers were hard at work on improvements, production of the tank was ramping up. A decree signed by the Council of Commissars and Central Committee of the Communist Party required the production of the first pilot series of T-34 tanks by the end of June of 1940, but as late as June 10 odds of satisfying this requirement appeared to be rather low. The ABTU's representative at factory #183 reported that production of specialized tools was just underway, with about 1,000 items scheduled to be completed by the end of June. Progress observed by June 25 was not encouraging: 1,400 items were designed, but no progress was made in actual production. Subcontractors dragged their heels: GAZ (Gorkiy Automotive Factory), STZ, GPZ #1 (State Ball Bearings Factory in Moscow), HTZ (Kharkov Tractor Factory) and Mariupol factory were all either late with their deliveries or not performing the work at all. For instance, STZ was supposed to deliver 11,100 cast track links by July 1, but had only delivered two hundred. Mariupol factory was supposed to begin casting DT machine-gun mount armour and final drive covers, but was refusing to perform the work entirely. It was a minor miracle that under these conditions factory #183 managed to assemble even four tanks in June instead of the requisite ten.

Meanwhile, the army's requirement for T-34 tanks was growing. The USSR was keeping an eye on current events, and it was clear that war with Germany was inevitable. As a result, factory #183's quota for 1940 more than doubled: from 200 to 500 T-34 tanks.[99] This new requirement did nothing to change the situation at the factory. The new quota of 20 tanks for July could not be met no matter how hard the army wished. As of July 15, the factory had ten hulls assembled to cover the shortfall from the previous month, and five hulls

ABOVE: *Stalinets* features a widened welded turret. The handrails are not original, and were likely installed during the tank's career as an observation post. *Patriot Park*

ABOVE: The gun maintenance hatch can be seen in the rear of the turret. This feature disappeared from T-34 tanks soon after the beginning of the war. The handrails welded to the engine deck are also not original. *Patriot Park*

available to satisfy July's quota. However, due to a shortage of other parts, only one T-34 was completed.[100]

The factory was not only behind on its production quota, but also efforts to expand production were not paying off. Even reduction of BT-7 tank output did not help matters. This kind of situation was unacceptable in the face of the coming war. An NKSM meeting was held in Moscow on July 23/24 to identify the cause of this delay. Makhonin outlined his list of complaints: the factory did not have sufficient raw materials or workforce to build new assembly lines, and subcontractors (chiefly STZ) were failing to deliver on their promises. The biggest issue was Mariupol factory's refusal to produce a number of cast armour components forcing factory #183 to set up its own casting operation, spreading its already scarce manpower even thinner. Anatoliy Nikolayevich Demyanovich, the director of STZ, objected, pointing out that factory #183 was at fault for failing to sign its contract with STZ on time. Surenyan and Goreglyad put an end to the unproductive finger-pointing. Ultimately, every party present carried some responsibility for the delays. The only solution was to stick to the production schedule set by the NKSM, which would ensure that each factory was sufficiently supplied with personnel and materials.[99] However, Fedorenko had no intention of letting factory #183 off easily. In order to ensure that quantity was not achieved at the expense of quality, the GABTU's representative at the factory, D. M. Kozyrev, was authorized to withhold payment if tanks were delivered with defects, or if known design flaws were not corrected.

This kind of coordination was easier said than done. Only two tanks were delivered in August instead of thirty. Some improvement was seen in September, with 37 tanks out of 80 delivered, but October was even worse: only one tank was completed out of a hundred and fifteen. Forty-five tanks were completed in five months of production, but it was clear that it would be a while before the entire production chain could master all of its new parts and processes. Instead of delivery to army units, the new tanks were put through extensive trials to discover manufacturing defects so that they could be corrected as quickly as possible. Assistance from the NII-48 research institute was required to teach welders how to work with austenitic electrodes. This degree of help had results. Thirty-eight tanks were completed in November (out of 120 planned), and by this point 35 were delivered to the end user. Thirty-two more were completed in December (out of 125) and 63 more were delivered. In total, the factory produced 125 tanks in 1940 (out of 500 planned) and

ABOVE: *Stalinets* retains its rectangular transmission access hatch in the upper rear plate, one of the most telling signs of an early T-34 tank. *Patriot Park*

delivered 108 of them. A slow start, to say the least.

Shortages of every single conceivable part were apparent. For instance, due to a shortage of track links shipped in from STZ, tracks had to be taken off tanks that went through the QA process and installed on freshly produced tanks so those could be tested as well.[102] The difficult situation with the subcontractors was further complicated by the fact that Morozov and his design bureau had to continuously introduce improvements to correct design defects that were identified during the trials of the A-34 prototypes, as well as new ones that cropped up during mass production. In order to keep production going at least to some degree, the correction of some issues was pushed back, some as far as the 750th or 1,000th tank produced. Based on the production rate that factory #183 could support, a T-34 tank that fully met the army's requirements would not be in production until the end of 1941, if not later.

Another issue arose at the end of 1940: finance. Despite popular belief, Stalin could not snap his fingers and set the price of goods and services to whatever he wished. The T-34 was a good example of this. According to decree #443ss, factory #183 would be paid 300,000 rubles for each new T-34 tank (not including the armament and sights, which were procured separately). However, the actual cost of a T-34 tank at the end of 1940 was more than double this number: 629,100 rubles. An investigation showed that the 'at cost' price was much lower, 433,146.53 rubles, but mark-up on parts purchased from subcontractors drove the price up significantly. Negotiations began between the many factories and organizations to drive down the cost of the tank. To compare, a BT-7M tank cost 138,705.04 rubles to make, less than a third of the price of even a discounted T-34.[103]

A meeting held at the People's Commissariat of Medium Machine Building (by then Vyacheslav Alexandrovich Malyshev had replaced Likhachev as People's Commissar) established that the quality of the assembled tanks had to be increased. Tanks still languishing at the factory were sifted through and the most acceptable ones picked out, resulting in acceptance of 135 tanks that were produced in 1940 and 31 tanks produced in January 1941, a total of 166 tanks. Tanks with the greatest amount of defects were singled out for trials, in order to determine the degree to which various issues impacted the tank's performance.[104] The rate of production kept increasing: 85 new tanks were completed in February and 134 in March. A revised production plan was published in March as well. The plan, signed on December 19, 1939, expected 1,600 tanks to be delivered in 1941 (668 with radios and 932 without), and actual production had to catch up. Three hundred tanks were due in the first quarter of 1941, perhaps the first production quota for T-34 tanks that factory #183 actually met: 385 tanks were delivered in this time interval, including leftovers from 1940.

Improvement in the rate of production continued under Malyshev's guidance. The quota for April was over-fulfilled: the factory delivered 140 instead of 125 tanks required of them. The over-achievement continued: in May 121 tanks were produced with 120 planned, and 170 tanks were produced in June with 140 planned.[105] The start of the German invasion of the Soviet Union on June 22 drastically changed both the planned and actual output of the factory.

Meanwhile, STZ was not faring as well as factory #183. Despite an initial requirement to produce only 20 T-34 tanks in 1940, the factory still lagged behind expectations. The cause was easy

Designing the T-34

to identify: factory #183 promised to send all blueprints pertaining to the new tanks in February 1940, but failed to meet that target. As of April 20, 1940, STZ had only received 1,400 blueprints out of 3,500. By June 20, it was clear that putting the tank into production would not be easy: 253 additional tools needed to be purchased before production could start. Construction work to build a new plant also had to be done, since the factory was initially equipped to produce the much smaller and lighter T-26 tank.

By August 19 the situation had not improved. Four hundred and two additional tools were identified as necessary for purchase, out of which only 57 had been received. New orders had come in from the NKSM regarding the delivery of the first 20 tanks by the end of October,[106] but that was not possible even if only parts produced at STZ were considered. As

ABOVE: The early driver's hatch contained a single observation device in the hatch itself and two more surrounding it. This allowed the driver to see across a 127-degree arc in front of the tank. A splash-proofing ridge runs along the perimeter of the hatch and the surrounding hull. *Patriot Park*

BELOW: Another view of the rear, showing the convoy light housing. The light itself is missing. *Patriot Park*

usual, subcontractors let the factory down: only six sets of hulls and turrets and five engines were delivered by September 19. No L-11 guns had been delivered at all. Furthermore, the required tools to bring the factory up to full production output had to be imported, but the import schedule stretched out well into 1942. This radically slowed down the rate of production.

The first two tanks were only completed and undergoing factory trials by mid-November. Four more were being prepared for trials and five were still in the process of assembly. Trials were complicated by the fact that the factory did not have a proper proving grounds and the closest artillery range was 80 km away. The first two tanks were deemed completed in January 1941. Twenty-eight tanks were built in February, and then 45 tanks in March (compared to the revised quota of thirty). Sixty-three tanks were built in April with 55 planned, 70 in May with 60 planned, and 86 in June with 75 planned. Despite a rocky start, the Stalingrad Tractor Factory was catching up.[107]

As could be expected, actual distribution of these tanks to army units lagged behind production. The first T-34 tanks to be issued arrived at the 8th Tank Division of the 4th Mechanized Corps: 20 on November 2, ten on November 8 and 20 on December 17. The 12th Tank Division of the 8th Mechanized Corps also received its first tanks in December of 1940, 30 in all. However, simply issuing a tank is not enough to turn it into a battle-ready asset. A GABTU commission that arrived to inspect these tanks in March 1941 discovered that each tank had only been run between seven and ten hours since they were received. Of all T-34s inspected in the Kiev and Baltic Special Military Districts, only four T-34s were driven for longer than 20 hours. Considering that an introductory course for a medium tank driver included five hours of practical exercise, it was clear

ABOVE: Radio antenna port in the right-hand side of the hull. *Patriot Park*

ABOVE: A road wheel and track grouser from a 1941-production T-34 tank. The rubber tyres heated up during high-speed marches in hot weather and required ventilation openings to stop them from overheating. *T-34 Tank Museum*

that, despite having been issued some time ago, these tanks were 'garage queens' that were not taken out for training.[108]

However, to simply say that these tanks were 'garage queens' would not be entirely accurate. A vital ingredient was missing: the garages. For instance, the 4th Mechanized Corps was in possession of 242 new T-34s as of May 1, 1941. Major General Andrei Vlasov, the corps commander, reported that his tank units were "packed in barracks very tightly, and do not have the necessary number of parks, garages, vegetable storages and lecture halls. Materiel is largely kept out in the open..."

This wasn't all: the 8th and 32nd Tank Divisions, the owners of these tanks, were desperately short of men. The 32nd Division was hurting the most, as it was missing 984 senior commanders, 1,268 junior commanders and 1,080 enlisted men, nearly a third of the total authorized strength. What men the division did have could not train with their tanks, since the division had not been allocated a shooting range or proving grounds after it was attached to the 4th Mechanized Corps and moved to Lvov. The division was also lacking all of the necessary support structures that go with tank units, such as field workshops, tools, etc. Under these

ABOVE: The first type of track link used on T-34 tanks, produced by stamping and welding. This type proved resilient, but time consuming to produce. *T-34 Tank Museum*

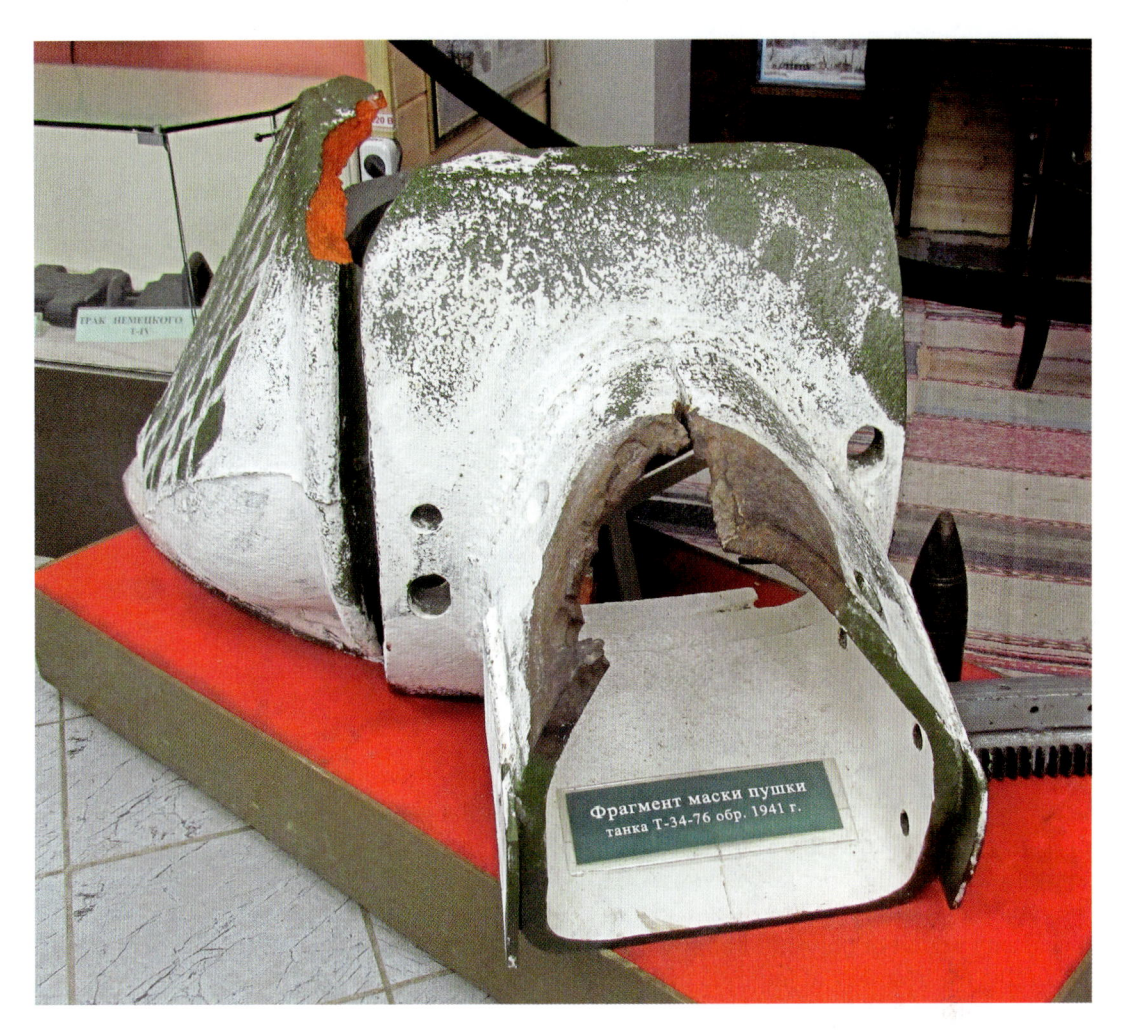

ABOVE: Fragments of a T-34 cast turret and F-34 gun mantlet. Winter 'tyre track' camouflage is applied, a common camouflage scheme. *T-34 Tank Museum*

conditions, it was no wonder that new T-34 tanks remained untouched: there were not enough people to drive them and nowhere to drive them to.[109] It was also not possible to learn the workings of the tank in theory: in addition to the aforementioned lack of classrooms, there were no manuals for L-10 and L-11 tank guns, and no manuals for the T-34 tank itself. The latter was only scheduled to be completed in November 1941.[110] This type of scenario was not the exception, but the rule. Due to a huge spike in the number of tankers in 1940/41, housing and training them all was proving to be an expensive and sluggish process. There was also a disproportionate number of rookies, and not enough experienced commanders and enlisted men to transfer over their knowledge.[111] Finally, commanders could not expect to receive enough spare parts to make up for wear and tear on their tanks during training, as the production plan for 1941 only satisfied 20 per cent of the emergency reserve requirement for spare parts. Some tank units would receive no spare parts at all until 1942, others only a miserly percentage of what was needed to keep their tanks running.[112] As of June 1,

ABOVE: Early type of cast track link. Mundane issues like a shortage of track links seriously interfered with T-34 production in 1940 and 1941. *T-34 Tank Museum*

1941, less than a month before the German invasion, 845 out of 892 T-34 tanks issued to the army had never been used.

In addition to not being able to train new tankers, letting new tanks sit idle led to another issue. Even the initial trials of A-20 and A-32 tanks showed that the limiting factor in the tank's service was the reliability of the engine, which had a warranty period of only 100 hours. Naturally, the best way to improve the lifespan of the engine was to study samples that broke and determine why the breakdown occurred, but coming across these samples was difficult. On June 18, 1941, the director of factory #75, Dmitriy Yermolayevich Kochetkov, pleaded with the GABTU and NKSM to allow his engineers to study the wear suffered by an engine over a period of 150–200 hours of use, even offering to accept all expenses associated with this experiment.[113] However, Kochetkov's proposal came too late. Only four days after his letter was written, Germany launched Operation *Barbarossa*, the invasion of the Soviet Union. A large number of tank projects, both prospective and those already in production, were axed to focus on a more manageable number of designs. Despite all of its drawbacks, the T-34 remained the backbone of the Red Army's tank units. The potential of the revolutionary design was clear. It would be some time before the T-34 would become "an engineering achievement of the first magnitude", but the groundwork for this achievement was already in place.

Glossary

A: The letter A at the start of a model number indicates a prototype vehicle built at factory #183. The index remained in use even after a tank entered production, for instance the BT-7 is called A-7 in factory documents.

ABTU: *Avto-bronetankovoye Upravleniye*, Automobile, Armoured Vehicle and Tank Directorate. Formed on November 22, 1934 to manage design and production of armoured and unarmoured vehicles for the army. Reformed into the GABTU (*Glavnoye Avto-bronetankovoye Upravleniye*, Main Automobile, Armoured Vehicle and Tank Directorate) on June 26, 1940.

Artillery Committee: A branch of the GAU in charge of artillery development. Sometimes referred to in documents as ArtKom or AK.

BT: *Bystrokhodniy Tank*, Fast Tank. Descendants of the Christie tank were referred to by this name, rather than the T-## nomenclature used for all other tanks.

Committee of Defence *see* KO

Factory #183: This factory began manufacturing military hardware in the early 1930s, producing many notable tanks, including the T-35, BT, and T-34. Its initial name, HPZ (Harkovskiy Paravozniy Zavod, Kharkov Locomotive Factory), was changed to 'factory #183' in 1937.

GABTU *see* ABTU

GAU: *Glavonoye Artilleriyeskoye Upravleniye*, Main Artillery Directorate. This organization was in charge of developing all sorts of artillery, including tank guns and SPGs.

GAZ: *Gorkiy Avtomobilniy Zavod*, Gorkiy Automotive Factory.

GlavSpetsMash: Main Directorate of Special Machine Building.

GPZ: *Gosudarstvenniy Podshipnikoviy Zavod*, State Ball Bearings Factory.

KO: *Komitet Oborony*, Committee of Defence within the Council of People's Commissars. This was the highest-ranking government body concerned with issues of defence.

Kubinka *see* NIBT Proving Grounds

RKKA: *Raboche-Krestyanskaya Krasnaya Armiya*, Worker and Peasant Red Army.

STZ: *Stalingradskiy Traktorniy Zavod*, Stalingrad Tractor Factory.

Mariupol factory: an armour producing factory in the Ukrainian city of Mariupol, honoured with Lenin's patronymic, sometimes just called Ilyich Factory in documents.

MZ: *Mariupolskiy Zavod*, Mariupol Factory. This index was used to refer to types of steel developed at this factory.

Glossary continued

NII-48: *Nauchno-Issledovatelniy Institut #48*, Scientific Research Institute #48. Specialized in armour research.

NIBT Proving Grounds: *Nauchno-Issledovatelniy Bronetakoviy Poligon*, Scientific Research Armoured Vehicle Proving Grounds. Located in Kubinka. Presently the site of the Kubinka Tank Museum and Patriot Park.

NKO: *Narodniy Kommissariat Oborony*, People's Commissariat of Defence.

NKOP: *Narodniy Kommissariat Oboronnoy Promyshlennosti*, People's Commissariat of Defence Industry.

NKSM: *Narodniy Kommissariat Sredney Promyshlennosti*, People's Commissariat of Medium Machine Building.

TPU: *Tankovoye Peregovornoye Ustroystvo*, Tank Intercom Device.

US: *Upravleniye Svyazi*, Communications Directorate of the ABTU and GABTU, dealing with the development of tank radios and intercoms.

VAMM: *Voyennaya Akademiya Mekhanizatsii i Motorizatsii*, Military Mechanization and Motorization Academy.

ZIS: *Zavod Imeni Stalina*, an automotive factory named after Stalin.

Notes

Introduction
1. Y. Belash, *Tanki Mezhvoyennogo Perioda*, Tactical Press, 2014 p. 148
2. Excerpt from minutes #40 of the Council of Labour and Defence, Tank building programme for 1929/1930 RGAE F.4372 Op.91 D.384 L.41
3. A. Solyankin et al, *Sovetskiye Lyogkiye Tanki 1920–1941*, Tseikhgauz, 2007 p. 6
4. Conclusions of the RKKA General Staff on the materials of the Directorate of Mechanization and Motorization of the RKKA on the assembly of armoured forces RGVA F.4 Op.14 D.628 L.8
5. S. Zaloga, *Spanish Civil War Tanks*, Osprey Publishing, 2010 p. 23
6. Y. Belash, *Tanki Mezhvoyennogo Perioda*, Tactical Press, 2014 p. 132
7. RGVA F.31811 Op.3 D.974 L.57-58
8. L. Vasilyeva et al, *Mihkail Koshkin: Unikalniye dokumenty, fotografii, fakty, i vospominaniya*, Izdat, 2008, pp. 19-20
9. RGVA F.4 Op.19 D.55 pp.1-9
10. A. Solyankin et al, *Sovetskiye Lyogkiye Tanki 1920–1941*, Tseikhgauz, 2007 pp. 10-11
11. Y. Belash, *Tanki Mezhvoyennogo Perioda*, Tactical Press, 2014 p. 146
12. RGVA F.31811 Op.3 D.974 L.1
13. RGVA F.4 Op.14. D.1897 L.115-125
14. I. Zheltov, A. Makarov, *Novoye Pravitelstvennoye Zadaniye* https://t34inform.ru/publication/p01-4.html
15. RGVA F.31811 Op.2 D.773 L.80
16. RGVA F.7719 Op.4 D.70 L.1-32
17. RGVA F.31811 Op.2 D.773 L157-159
18. RGVA F.31811 Op.2 D.773 L.156
19. RGVA F.31811 Op.2 D.773 L.215
20. RGVA F.31811 Op.2 D.842 L.21-36
21. RGVA F.7515 Op.1 D.321 L.46

Two Tanks for the Price of One
22. RGVA F.31811 Op.2 D.842 L.263-315
23. I. Zheltov, A. Makarov, *Osnovnoye oruzhie pervykh tridtsatchtrverok, Dokumentalno-istoricheskiy sbornik #2*
24. I. Zheltov, A. Makarov, *Ot proyektov k opytmym obraztsam*
25. RGVA F.4 Op.18 D.46 L.259
26. GARF F.R-8418 Op.28 D.39 L.152
27. RGAE F.8115 Op.8 D.16 L.18-19
28. RGVA F.31811 Op.2 D.888 L.49
29. RGVA F.31811 Op.2 D.888 L.52
30. RGVA F.31811 Op.3 D.1633 L.9
31. RGVA F.4 Op.14 D.2222 L.11-14
32. RGVA F.31811 Op.3 D.1633 L.16-19
33. RGVA F.31811 Op.3 D.1633 L.97
34. RGVA F.31811 Op.3 D.1633 L.4
35. RGVA F.4 Op.14 D.2222 L.11-14
36. RGVA F.31811 Op.3 D.1633 L.97
37. I. Zheltov, A. Makarov, Khronika ispytaniy tankov A-20 i A-32
38. RGVA F.31811 Op.3 D.1633 L.15
39. RGVA F.4 Op.14 D.2222 L.30-35
40. I. Zheltov, A. Makarov, *A-34 Rozhdeniye Tridtsatchetverki* p. 11

Bigger and Better
41. RGVA F.31811 Op.3 D,1633 L.110
42. RGVA F.31811 Op.3 D.1633 L.375-376
43. I. Zheltov, A. Makarov, *A-34 Rozhdeniye Tridtsatchetverki* pp. 35-9
44. I. Zheltov, A. Makarov, *A-34 Rozhdeniye Tridtsatchetverki* p. 15
45. I. Zheltov, A. Makarov, *A-34 Rozhdeniye Tridtsatchetverki* p. 17
46. I. Zheltov, A. Makarov, *A-34 Rozhdeniye Tridtsatchetverki* pp. 19-26
47. I. Zheltov, A. Makarov, *A-34 Rozhdeniye Tridtsatchetverki* pp. 34-5
48. I. Zheltov, A. Makarov, *A-34 Rozhdeniye Tridtsatchetverki* p. 41
49. I. Zheltov, A. Makarov, *A-34 Rozhdeniye Tridtsatchetverki* pp.130-1
50. I. Zheltov, A. Makarov, *A-34 Rozhdeniye Tridtsatchetverki* p. 45
51. RGAE F.7914 Op.1 D.26 L.1-9
52. I. Zheltov, A. Makarov, *A-34 Rozhdeniye Tridtsatchetverki* pp. 132-8
53. I. Zheltov, A. Makarov, *A-34 Rozhdeniye Tridtsatchetverki* pp.139-46
54. I. Zheltov, A. Makarov, *A-34 Rozhdeniye Tridtsatchetverki* pp.159-60
55. L. Vasilyeva et al, *Mihkail Koshkin: Unikalniye*

Notes continued

dokumenty, fotografii, fakty, i vospominaniya, Izdat, 2008, p. 107

From A to T

56 RGVA F.31811 Op.2 D.1181 L.98
57 I. Zheltov, A. Makarov, *A-34 Rozhdeniye Tridtsatchetverki* pp.188-208
58 I. Zheltov, A. Makarov, *Nachalo Osvoyeniya Seriynogo Proizvodtva Tankov T-34*
59 A. Makarov, *Sredniy tank T-34: Razvitiye bronevoy zaschty v 1939–1943 gg*
60 RGVA F.31811 Op.2 D.1181 L.116
61 RGVA F.31811 Op.2 D.1181 L.106-107
62 I. Zheltov, A. Makarov, *Nachalo Osvoyeniya Seriynogo Proizvodtva Tankov T-34*
63 I. Zheltov, A. Makarov, *A-34 Rozhdeniye Tridtsatchetverki* p. 216
64 TsAMO RF F.38 Op.11355 D.41 L.12-13
65 TsAMO RF F.38 Op.11355 D.232 L.21-27
66 A. Makarov, *Sredniy tank T-34: Razvitiye bronevoy zaschty v 1939–1943 gg*
67 RGVA F.31811 Op.2 D.1022 L.94-95
68 RGVA F.31811 Op.2 D.1181 L.201-204
69 TsAMO RF F.38 Op.11355 D.41 L.10-11
70 A. Makarov, *Sredniy tank T-34: Razvitiye bronevoy zaschty v 1939–1943 gg*
71 RGVA F.31811 Op.2 D.1068 L.1-157
72 RGVA F.31811 Op.2 D. 1022 L.312-315
73 RGVA F.31811 Op.2 D.1129 L.208-209
74 RGVA F.31811 Op.2 D.1181 L.133
75 RGVA F.31811 Op.2 D.1130 L.31-32
76 RGVA F.31811 Op.2 D.1130 L.67-79
77 RGVA F.31811 Op.2 D.1130 L.175-178
78 RGVA F.31811 Op.2 D.1068 L.1-157
79 RGVA F.31811 Op.3 D.1873 L.1-5
80 V. Podepenets, *Istoriya tankovoy radiostantsii 10RT-26*
81 TsAMO RF F.38 Op.11355 D.41 L.230-231
82 http://tankarchives.blogspot.com/2013/05/penetration-part-3.html
83 RGVA F.31811 Op.2 D.978 L.253-254
84 RGVA F.31811 Op.2 D.978 L.321
85 RGVA F.31811 Op.2 D.1186 L.95-97
86 http://tankarchives.blogspot.com/2013/05/penetration-part-3.html
87 TsAMO RF F.38 Op.11355 D.41 L.19-22
88 TsAMO RF F.38 Op.11355 D.178 L.1-20
89 A. G. Solyankin et al, *Sredniy Tank T-34 1939–1945,* p. 44
90 RGASPI F.644 Op.1 D.2 L.36-38
91 RGVA F.31811 Op.2 D.1068 L.1-157
92 TsAMO RF F.38 Op.11355 D.41 L.10-11
93 I. Zheltov, A. Makarov, *A-34 Perviye Tridtsatchetverki* pp. 220-9
94 Tank Archives, New Year New Engine
95 Y. Pasholok, *Vremennoye Usileniye*
96 RGVA F.31811 Op.3 D.2116 L.1-100

Production and Service

97 https://vif2ne.org/nvk/forum/archive/2870/2870097.htm
98 Y. Pasholok, *T-34 iz ekspozitsii TsM BTVT*
99 GARF F.R-5446 Op.1v D.523 L.216-224
100 RGVA F.31811 Op.2 D.1181 L.155-156
101 RGAE F.8115 Op.8 D.15 L.154-166
102 RGVA F.31811 Op.2 D.1068 L.1-157
103 I. Zheltov, A. Makarov, *Podvodya itogi predvoyennogo goda*
104 TsAMO RF F.38 Op.11355 D.41 L.47-49
105 A. Ulanov, D. Shein, *Perviye T-34*, pp. 36-52
106 GARF F.R-5446 Op.1v D.523 L.216-224
107 A. Ulanov, D. Shein, *Perviye T-34*, pp. 53-61
108 A. Ulanov, D. Shein, *Perviye T-34*, pp. 61-3
109 A. Ulanov, D. Shein, *Perviye T-34*, pp. 67-71
110 http://tankarchives.blogspot.com/2016/01/plans-for-1941.html
111 A. Ulanov, D. Shein, *Perviye T-34*, p. 82
112 TsAMO RF F.38 Op.11355 D.225 L.69
113 TsAMO RF F.38 Op.11355 D.138 L.150

Index

ABTU (Automobile, Armoured Vehicle and Tank Directorate) *also* GABTU 11, 12,14, 16, 17, 23, 34, 42, 54, 57-60, 63-67, 76, 78, 81, 84
Arman, Paul Matisovich 11
Artillery Committee 55

Bokis, Gustav Gustavovich 14, 15
Bondarenko, director 15-17
Budyonny, Semyon 23

Christie, Walter 15, 16, 18
Committee of Defence *also* KO 12, 24, 38, 51, 63
Council of Commissars of the USSR 38, 51, 76
Council of People's Commissars 7, 70

Demyanovich, Anatoliy Nikolayevich 77
Dik, Adolf Yakovlevich 14

factories
    #8 60
    #37 (Moscow) 17, 44
    #75 84
    #92 67
    #174 (Leningrad) 11, 37
    #183 (formerly Kharkov Locomotive Factory (HPZ)) 11, 13, 14, 15, 17, 21, 23-25, 29, 31, 34, 36-39, 43, 51, 53, 58, 60, 63, 67, 70, 75-77, 79, 80
    #185 17
    GAZ (Gorkiy Automotive Factory) 76
    GPZ (State Ball Bearings Factory, Moscow) 76
    HTZ (Kharkov Tractor Factory) 76
    Kirov 36, 55
    Mariupol *also* MZ 25, 27, 35, 36, 57, 58, 60, 67, 76, 77
    STZ (Stalingrad Tractor Factory) 14, 29, 34, 37, 39, 51, 76, 77, 79, 80
Farmanyants, K. P.
Fedorenko, director 63, 77

GABTU *see* ABTU
GAU (Main Artillery Directorate) 63
GlavSpetsMash (Main Directorate of Special Machine Building) 50

Goreglyad, Aleksey Adamovich 25, 43, 51, 77
Great Patriotic War 7, 9
Kaganovich, Mikhail Moiseevich 15, 16
Kochetkov, Dmitriy Yermolayevich 84
Koshkin, Mikhail Ilyich 11, 16, 23, 25, 36, 43, 51, 53
Kozyrev, D. M. 78
Krivoshein, Semyon Moiseevich 10, 11
Kubinka proving grounds 29, 44, 71
Kulik, Grigoriy Ivanovich 39, 50

Likhachev, Ivan Alekseevich 24, 25, 29, 36, 37, 51, 79

Makhonin, Sergei Nestorovich 37, 77
Maksarev, Yuri Evgeniyevich 34, 36, 63
Malyshev, Vyacheslav Alexandrovich 30, 79
Mekhlis, Lev 23
Mikoyan, Anastas 29
Morozov, Alexander Alexandrovich 16, 23, 25, 53, 56, 66, 79

NIBT proving grounds 44
NII-20 (Scientific Research Institute #20) 65
NII-48 (Scientific Research Institute #48) 60, 78
NKO (People's Commissariat of Defence) 31, 50
NKOP (People's Commissariat of Defence Industry) 15, 17, 23
NKSM (People's Commissariat of Medium Machine Building) 24, 38, 77, 80, 84

Operation *Barbarossa* 84

Panov, Maj I. G. 31
Parfenov, director 17
Pavlov, Dmitriy Grigoryevich 12, 17, 23, 28, 29, 31, 34, 36, 37, 50, 57, 58

Red Army 6-8, 11-14, 17, 23, 34, 35, 38, 56, 74, 75, 84
    4th Mechanized Corps 81, 82
        8th Tank Division 81
    8th Mechanized Corps 81
        12th Tank Division 81
        32nd Tank Division 82
RKKA *see* Red Army

Index continued

Sorokin, R. E. 55
Spanish Civil War 8, 9, 18
Stalin, Joseph 23, 37, 50, 79
Surenyan, G. S. 50, 77
Sviridov, D. V. 15-17

tanks (foreign)
    Christie *also* M.1940 8, 12-16
    CV 3/35 (tankette) 8
    Pz.Kpfw.I 8
    Renault FT 7
tanks (Soviet) prototypes and T-34 precursors
    A-20 7, 18-31, 34, 37-39, 47, 50, 84
    A-20 (tracked) *also* A-20G 21-23, 25
    A-32 22, 25-32, 34, 35, 37-39, 43, 47, 48, 50, 66, 84
    A-34 32-44, 48-50, 53, 56, 58, 59, 63, 66, 69, 71, 79
    BT-5 8, 15, 16, 55
    BT-7 11, 12, 16, 19, 20, 21, 26-28, 36, 44, 66, 77
    BT-7-B-IS 11
    BT-7M 20, 26-28, 79
    BT-20 12, 17, 19
KV-1 55, 63
    MS-1 7, 8
    T-26 8, 10, 11, 12, 15, 17, 20, 34, 38, 39, 66, 80
    T-28 12-14, 34
    T-29 11-14
    T-35 11, 12, 34
    T-46 11
    T-46-3 11
Timoshenko, Semyon Konstantinovich 57
Tsyganov, N. F. 10

VAMM (Military Mechanization and Motorization Academy) 14, 15
Vlasov, Maj Gen Andrei 82
Voroshilov, Kliment 9-12, 23, 29, 50, 57
Voroshilovets tractor 39, 43

Worker and Peasant Red Army (RKKA) *see* Red Army

Zhdanov, Andrei 29